Floria

T0270242

111 Places
in Napa and Sonoma
That You Must
Not Miss

Photographs by Steve Werney

emons:

Bibliographical information of the Deutsche Nationalbibliothek
The Deutsche Nationalbibliothek lists this publication in
the Deutsche Nationalbibliografie; detailed bibliographical data
are available on the internet at http://dnb.d-nb.de.

© Emons Verlag GmbH
All rights reserved
© Photographs by Steve Werney, except see page 239
© Cover icon: shutterstock/PRAPHAN BUNMAO
Layout: Eva Kraskes, based on a design
by Lübbeke | Naumann | Thoben
Maps: altancicek.design, www.altancicek.de
Basic cartographical information from Openstreetmap,
© OpenStreetMap-Mitwirkende, OdbL
Edited by: Karen E. Seiger
Printing and binding: Grafisches Centrum Cuno, Calbe
Printed in Germany 2024
ISBN 978-3-7408-1553-0
First edition

Guidebooks for Locals & Experienced Travelers
Join us in uncovering new places around the world at
www.111places.com

Foreword

While you surely think of Napa and Sonoma Counties as the heart of California Wine Country, I'm happy to tell you that there is much, much more to this region. Of course food and wine are important, and I've included a select few wineries and restaurants for their unique and compelling stories. However, this book is mostly about the other places here that you must see, experience, and remember.

This region is powered by agricultural wealth, innovation, and fabulous coastal landscapes. Beginning with Native Americans who have lived here for centuries, the local environment encourages all sorts of iconoclasts and creatives. Small towns are filled with crafters and artists. Local roadhouses are alive with music, and farms and hot springs abound.

And sometimes, a new, unexplored place creates an unanticipated connection to another place or perspective you've long forgotten. For me, it was the Quixote Winery, a strange and bewitching place in Napa Valley. It was designed largely by the Austrian architect, artist, sculptor, and free thinker Friedensreich Hundertwasser. He's well known in Europe, but this project was his only one in the United States. I first saw his work while an art student in Vienna, and I was struck by his fearless creativity. While researching this book, I was reminded of him again.

Many others have found inspiration here, such as writer Jack London and his wife Charmian; Gonzo journalist Hunter Thompson; photographer and activist Lisa Kristine; Carlo Marchiori and his magical Villa Ca'toga; philanthropist Nan Tucker McEvoy; and Mary Ellen Pleasant, the Rosa Parks of San Francisco. It's the incredible people here, with their deep affection for and dependence on the land, who inspired me to write this book. I hope you'll want to return to Napa and Sonoma Counties many times to encounter the work and contributions of those who have given this region its distinct character and energy.

111 Places

1 *Ars Longa Vita Brevis*
Napa's history in a mosaic

At the historic Mill in Riverbend plaza in downtown Napa, you'll find a two-tiered mosaic fountain entitled *Ars Longa Vita Brevis*, meaning "Life is Brief, Art Endures." The vibrant artwork, completed by prominent local artist Alan Shepp in 2005, is made of smalti mosaic tiles imported from Italy and depicts scenes from the city's history, both the glory and the ignominy. The mosaic is part of a rich public art tradition in Northern California.

Alan Shepp is a multimedia artist, who works out of his studio in Napa Valley. He often creates with stone; his slate sculptures possess airiness and movement. You can see his art in exhibits at the Di Rosa Center For Contemporary Art among other places.

Shepp's work in Napa was two years in the making, and it's separated into two parts. The upper section portrays the history of Napa Valley's role in the settlement of the West. You'll see agricultural scenes from the 19th century, along with scenes of Spanish, Mexican, and Chinese workers. In an interview with the *Napa Valley Register* in 2005, Shepp said, "I gave the Chinese a prominent place [in the mosaic]. They're the ones who cleared the valley and dug the caves at two cents a day." The bottom section of the mosaic includes Napa River flora and fauna. Look for various fish, turtles, and a beaver, as well as sunken boats. Tiles designed as a "living river" flow from the fountain onto the plaza and offer a spectacular effect at night, when they reflect the lights.

The mosaic became controversial shortly after it was unveiled because of visual references to two Ku Klux Klan initiation rallies in the mid 1930s. Large crosses were burned, and the events drew thousands of onlookers. The National Association for the Advancement of Colored People (NAACP) suggested that Shepp use their circular blue logo to obscure all but some flames and the outlines of white hoods, and that's what you see today.

Address 500 Main Street, Napa, CA 94559, +1 (707) 251-8500, historicnapamill.com | Getting there By car, from CA-221 N / Soscol Avenue, turn left onto 3rd Street and then left onto Main Street to the destination. | Hours Unrestricted | Tip At the Napa Mill, established in 1884 by Captain Albert Hatt, you will find live entertainment, restaurants, wine tasting, a variety of other shops, and the historic Napa River Inn (500 Main Street, Napa, www.napariverinn.com).

2 Bale Grist Mill

An early form of green technology

Grist mills are one of the great technological advancements in human history, comparable to the sail. They have been around since the third century BC. They may have been invented in what is now Turkey. Over the millennia, they've been powered by slaves, livestock, furnaces, water (including wastewater), and wind. In 1300, there were 17,000 such mills in England. Today, there are more than two dozen still in use in the United States. Only one still operates west of the Mississippi: the Bale Grist Mill, three miles north of Saint Helena.

It was built in 1846 by Edward Bale, who sailed from England to California in the 1830s. He eventually was named surgeon-in-chief of the Mexican Army by General Mariano Vallejo. In 1839, Bale married Vallejo's niece and was granted a ranch south of Calistoga in 1841. He built the mill to serve a 10-mile radius for farmers, settlers, and prospectors looking to have their corn and wheat milled into meal or flower. Because of the slow rotation of the grindstone and the dampness of the mill itself, the mill acquired a singular reputation for cornbread, yellow bread, shortening bread, and spoonbread.

The actual grinding involved two very large round stones imported from a quarry north of Paris. They were separated by the width of a sheet of paper. Just a minute amount of separation is important because otherwise the grinding process may burn the corn; hence the occasional need to sniff for the scent of cooked corn. There was another reason to ensure separation, which was that the grinding could produce a lot of grit which wore down the enamel on teeth when baked into the bread.

The mill and its 36-foot water wheel comprise a state historic landmark and have been partly restored. Milling demonstrations and tours take place on weekends. You can buy freshly milled flour, and all proceeds go to preserving the mill.

Address 3369 Saint Helena Highway N, Saint Helena, CA 94574, +1 (707) 942-4575, www.napaoutdoors.org/parks/bale-grist-mill-state-historic-park | Getting there By car, take CA-29 N three miles past Saint Helena. The destination will be on the left. | Hours Sat & Sun 10am–4pm | Tip To experience a medieval Italian castle, visit Castello di Amorosa, which has all the typical architectural elements of a castle, including a moat, a drawbridge, a chapel, and five towers (4045 Saint Helena Highway, Calistoga, www.castellodiamorosa.com).

3 — Calistoga Pioneer Cemetery
History interred

You'll find Calistoga Pioneer Cemetery a mile north of downtown Calistoga. The graves, set in among Valley Oaks, dried moss, and wild vinca vines, are spread over five acres along a steep hillside. Now unkempt, the grounds were set aside in the 1870s. The cemetery has 948 known graves, along with an unknown number of unmarked graves, as so many records have been lost. The headstones display the names of farmers, craftsmen, and veterans of the Grand Army of the Republic. Look for the seven-foot-tall, wooden obelisk for unknown soldiers.

There's the grave of Suzanne Reid, a Midwestern landowner's daughter who turned down a marriage proposal from Abraham Lincoln because he was "goofy looking" and eventually settled in Calistoga. There's a woman thought to be a member of the local Wappo tribe buried next to a man whose wife is buried somewhere else. There are Mexican markers, but no known graves of Black people. And then there's Eli "Bud" Philpott, a stagecoach driver from Calistoga killed in a gold bullion robbery in Arizona in March 1881. Several months later, lawmen, including the Earp Brothers, confronted the robbers in Tombstone in what became known as the Gunfight at the O.K. Corral.

Among pioneers in the cemetery are members of the Donner-Reed Party, including the Graves and Cyrus families. Eighty-seven people set off in April, 1846 from Independence, Missouri. Only 47 reached the Sacramento Valley. They took what they were assured was a shortcut to California, but they ended up at Truckee Lake, trapped by a series of snowstorms. It's a tale of bad luck, heroism, murder, cannibalism, and survival, reflecting the "brunt of fate," according to a memorial plaque along the route.

The cemetery grounds are very steep, and vehicles are not allowed to the upper sections without a permit. So take your time as you wander among the graves.

Address 2001-2219 Foothill Boulevard, Calistoga, CA 94515 | Getting there By car, from CA-29, take Foothill Boulevard in Calistoga to the destination. | Hours Daily 8am–6pm | Tip Nearby Tank Garage Winery offers a sparkling Barbera called "Ancestral Maneuvers in the Dark" and more in their preserved 1930s gas station (1020 Foothill Boulevard, Calistoga, www.tankgaragewinery.com).

4__ Chateau Montelena
Wrapped in Jade

The Judgment of Paris event in 1976 was a huge deal at the time, although later its legacy was stained by myths, a few drops of bad blood, and a panned film called *Bottle Shock*. The original story was that Steven Spurrier, a British wine merchant and owner of a wine shop in Paris, wanted to sponsor a wine competition to promote French wines. Another story is that a close friend of Spurrier's named Patricia Gastaud-Gallagher came up with the idea. She would later claim she merely wanted to commemorate the American bicentennial with an educational blind tasting – a "friendly," as it were.

Naturally, the French wines were expected to dominate. Eleven French judges carried out two blind comparisons: one among Chardonnays, and the other of Bordeaux wines from France and Cabernet Sauvignon wines from Napa. The judges rated the Napa wines as the best in each category. One of the judges, the very distinguished Odette Kahn, was so incensed that she renounced her ballot, denounced Spurrier, and cried foul to the press. But the victory was no fluke. Blind tastings in 1986 and the 30th anniversary competition in 2006 affirmed the original conclusions.

The winner of the 1976 Chardonnay tasting was Chateau Montelena (vintage 1973). Founded in 1882, it's one of the oldest wineries in Napa County and one of the two great vineyards from the Carneros region.

Chateau Montelena has become best known for its own Cabernet Sauvignons and for the vineyard itself, which is anchored by a moody, gothic castle and Jade Lake. The lake was created in 1958 by then owners Yort Wing-Frank, an electrical engineer from China, and his wife Jeanie. They wanted to create a picturesque home for their retirement and added the lake with an island that hosts a garden and pavilion. The island is connected to the shore by beautifully crafted zigzagging bridges designed to keep the evil spirits away.

Address 1429 Tubbs Lane, Calistoga, CA 94515, +1 (707) 942-5105, www.montelena.com, service@montelena.com | Getting there By car, from CA-29, take Tubbs Lane in Calistoga to the destination. | Hours Gardens daily 9:30am–4pm | Tip On the way, you must stop at the Old Faithful Geyser of California (1299 Tubbs Lane, Calistoga, www.oldfaithfulgeyser.com).

5 Chuck Williams Culinary Art Museum

The beauty of cookware

It's mid-afternoon on a weekday, and two women are standing outside the Chuck Williams Culinary Arts Museum, on the second floor of the Culinary Institute of America (CIA) in Napa. It's as clean and well-lit a place as you'll ever find, and a sanctuary for anyone longing to be around the particular beauty of kitchen instruments, some dating back to the mid 18th century. There are pots, kettles, saucepans, knives, platters, every kind of tureen you could ever imagine, some in the form of boar's heads, rabbits, and lambs, and specialty items like a duck press, as well as spic-and-span vintage gas ovens. "Sometimes, I'll just come here in the middle of the day to look at all these beautiful things," one woman says to the other. "And I'll say to myself, 'Just keep going toward the beauty, and eventually you'll get there.'"

Chuck Williams died in 2015 at 100 years old. He was the founder of an "era of aspirational culinary retailing" in the mid 1950s and created a small empire of upper-end stores and services. He grew up in Palm Springs during the Depression and later lived in Los Angeles. He was fascinated by food and cooking, and in 1953, he made an especially informative trip to France and other parts of Western Europe, where he went from shop to shop, restaurant to restaurant, and factory to factory, researching and acquiring top-of-the-line kitchenware. He then opened his first store in Sonoma in 1956 in a converted hardware shop. It was wildly popular and eventually would become Williams-Sonoma, the nation-wide cooking and entertainment store. He created the name by combining his own last name with the place where he opened the first store.

The museum in downtown Napa grew out of Williams' personal collection and includes some 4,000 items.

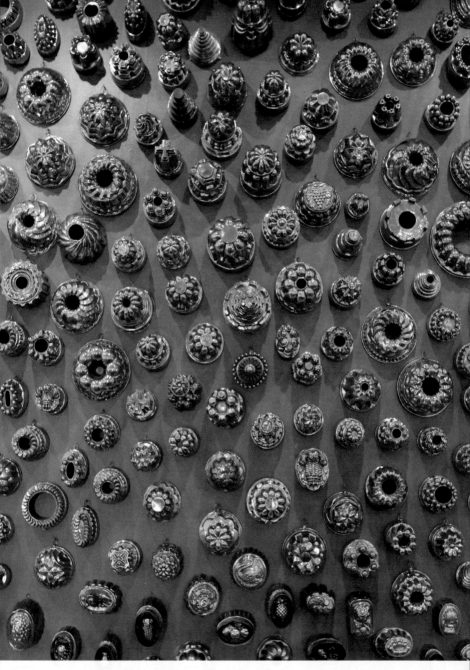

Address 500 1st Street, Napa, CA 94559, +1 (707) 967-2500, www.ciaatcopia.com | Getting there By car, from CA-29, turn onto 1st Street in Napa. | Hours Daily 11am–5pm | Tip On the first floor of the CIA, you'll find the Marketplace, full of beautiful household items for your own kitchen (www.ciaatcopia.com/marketplace).

6 Di Rosa Center for Contemporary Art

An exquisite art park

Rene di Rosa arrived at Yale in 1930. His father was an Italian aristocrat, and his mother an heiress from St. Louis. He served in World War II and afterwards tried out a bohemian writer's life in Paris. When a novel wouldn't come, he flew to San Francisco and got a job as a reporter. But he finally decided instead to explore an existence "closer to Mother Nature and Father Soil."

Di Rosa and his wife Veronica, a Canadian artist well known for her steel sculptures, were absolutely unwilling to abide by convention. It was while learning the art of growing grapes at UC Davis that he fell into the world of artists, which included Robert Arneson, Roy De Forest, Manuel Neri, and William T. Wiley. He would establish the di Rosa Center for Contemporary Art, devoted to the works of "emerging talent," above all, mid 20th and early 21st century Northern California talent. He expanded a small pond into a 35-acre lake, which became the core of his museum. di Rosa once said that he saw himself as someone who could help others become the artist he had failed to become.

Others in the permanent collection include Mildred Howard, artist and activist, perhaps best known for her *Bottle Houses*, which she called "vessels of memory." You'll find one by Gallery 2. She explains on the Turner Carrol Gallery website that she was "exploring the physics of light. I always knew there were bottle houses in the south. They used bottles to decorate trees and to keep bad spirits away. I was interested in what happens when light hits a bottle throughout the day."

The museum includes two galleries, a sculpture meadow, and an olive grove, and contains more than 1800 works by 600 artists. At any one time, there may be nearly 80 works on exhibit. You can also join guided hikes through the property.

Address 5200 Sonoma Highway, Napa, CA 94559, +1 (707) 226-5991, www.dirosaart.org, visit@dirosaart.org | Getting there By car, from CA-29, take CA-121 W to the destination. | Hours Fri–Sun 11am–4pm | Tip Located just across the Sonoma Highway is Domaine Carneros, founded by the French champagne house of Taittinger, where you can enjoy their sparkling wines (1240 Duhig Road, Napa, www.domainecarneros.com).

7 Dr. Wilkinson's

Home of an original mud bath treatment

In 1952, "Doc" John and Edy Wilkinson were two Calistoga characters, or you could say "pleasurists," who opened the now historic Dr. Wilkinson's Backyard Resort and Mineral Springs. Their innovation was to popularize mud baths, a source of pleasure and healing used by the local Wappo tribe for centuries, if not millennia, but not widely used in US resorts in the 1950s.

The Wilkinsons had only the most modest of backgrounds in the hydrotherapy arts. Doc was a chiropractor and had worked briefly in spas. He also served as Calistoga's mayor at one point. Edy was an artist who specialized in glass and tile mosaics. If they knew little about the virtues of mud when they first embarked on this new venture in health and wellness, the Wilkinsons were quick learners and good promoters.

They would become known as "wellness experts," and they developed a "secret formula" for their mud baths, which to this day is kept in a notebook under lock and key. The formula is partly derived from a blend of Canadian peat moss, mineral water from local wells, and volcanic ash from Mt. Saint Helena. During treatment, the mud is kept at 107 degrees Fahrenheit.

The Wilkinsons worked only when they wanted, when there was pleasure in it. Sometimes, Doc would go out into the street and engage passersby, talking them up about the health benefits of mud. He was endlessly congenial and attracted a loyal following.

He developed a product line of massages and baths. One of the spa's signature treatments has always been "The Works," which includes a mud bath thermo-therapy and face mask, a soak in a mineral water hydrotherapy pool, a rest in a sleep-inducing cool blanket wrap, and finally, a half-hour massage. The Wilkinson family sold the resort in 2021. The venue, which has 50 rooms, was renovated and maintains its mid-20th century ambiance.

Address 1507 Lincoln Avenue, Calistoga, CA 94515, +1 (707) 942-4102, www.drwilkinson.com, info@drwilkinson.com | Getting there By car, from CA-29, take Lincoln Avenue in Calistoga to the destination. | Hours By appointment only | Tip If you're hungry for French cuisine served on a patio under orange trees, then you'll enjoy Evangeline, located in Calistoga City Hall (1226 Washington Street, Calistoga, www.evangelinenapa.com).

8 Falconry at Bouchaine Vineyards

The musings of raptors

Los Carneros is a region that runs along the southern tip of Napa Valley. It's where the Mayacamas Mountains disappear into San Pablo Bay, and it's distinguished by cool, sometimes foggy weather – perfect for growing grapes for pinot noir, Chardonnay, and sparkling wines. There are some 20 wineries in Los Carneros, spread over 90 square miles. The oldest is the Bouchaine Vineyards, first planted in the 1880s.

In recent years, Bouchaine, a family-owned vineyard on 100 acres, has drawn attention for using highly trained falcons, eagles, and hawks to ward off various grape eaters, notably crows, songbirds, and particularly starlings, which ravage vine clusters. The only natural countermeasure to starlings is birds of prey. One of the companies in the forefront of this strategy is Authentic Abatement, founded by Rebecca Rosen, a falcon whisperer and long-time raptor advocate with a particular interest in ethical issues. She began working with Bouchaine in 2016.

In July through October, Rosen arrives at a vineyard in her black truck. She launches a bird chosen for a particular setting and repeats the pattern every day for two weeks of "solid harassment," as Rosen puts it. "My truck becomes identified with the predator." The sight and sound of her truck alone gradually become sufficient means to dispel the starlings.

Bouchaine offers raptor demonstrations during which vineyard guests can take videos and photos with the birds. Rosen offers a masterclass on training these birds: on their similarity to humans, particularly when it comes to remembering human faults and slights; on how hawks sometimes hunt as a family; and on the utter devotion of many raptors to their offspring. Call the winery to join a "Falconry in the Garden" event.

Address 1075 Buchli Station Road, Napa, CA 94559, +1 (707) 252-9065, www.bouchaine.com, info@bouchaine.com | Getting there By car, from CA-121, take Buhig Road S, then turn left onto Las Amigas Road and left onto Buchli Station Road to the destination. | Hours See website for event information and reservations | Tip Just beyond the vineyards, you can take a stroll among the yachts, and shop in the chandlery and grocery store at Napa Valley Marina (1200 Milton Road, Napa, www.napavalleymarina.com).

9 Far Niente Winery

Where vintage refers to both wine and historic race cars

Far Niente Winery's name is a reference to the Italian concept of "the pleasure of doing nothing." The winery was established in Oakville in 1885 by a Gold Rush baron named John Benson. Interestingly, Benson's nephew was Winslow Homer, the American landscape painter known for his ocean scenes. Benson hired Hamden McIntyre to be the architect for his winery. McIntyre was the leading local authority on designing gravity-flow wineries, in which gravity moved the grapes through the entire production process. He would design many of the valley's great wineries.

When Prohibition was unleashed in 1919, Far Niente was quickly ruined and then abandoned for 60 years – until 1979, when Gil Nickel bought the business and brought it back to life in 1982. The vineyard is best known for Chardonnays and Cabernet Sauvignons. Nickel had grown up in Oklahoma, in a family that made a fortune in the nursery business. Nickel stayed with the family business until 1976, when he pursued his interest in oenology at UC Davis. From there, he set his eye on Far Niente.

But at the same time, Nickel followed a companion interest: auto racing, specifically with historic European sports cars. In 1984, he began racing in earnest, and in 1995 he became the first American to win the European FIA Historic Sports Car Championship. He was driving a 1962 Lotus 23B. He continued to compete almost until his death in 2003. Through the years, he acquired an extraordinary collection of cars, which are kept at the winery in a large stable known as "Gil's Place."

The collection includes, among others, a 1966 Ferrari 500 Superfast, a 1961 Corvette roadster, and a perfectly kept 1935 Bentley 3.5 liter Sports Saloon. However, the pride of Nickel's collection is a 1951 Ferrari 340 America with the famous Vignale body. He was charmed by the car's perfect design. It's the car he often drove at Sonoma Raceway.

Address 1350 Acacia Drive, Oakville, CA 94562, +1 (707) 944-2861, www.farniente.com, info@farniente.com | **Getting there** By car, from CA-29, take Oakville Grade Road two miles north of Yountville, and then turn left onto Acacia Drive. | **Hours** By appointment | **Tip** Visit the Olive Mill at Round Pond, one of two working olive mills in Napa County (886 Rutherford Road, Rutherford, www.roundpond.com).

10___French Laundry's Garden

Straight from the garden to your table

The French Laundry, located in a charming two-story stone cottage, is an exclusive and internationally renowned restaurant located just 15 minutes north of Napa. It opened in 1994, and in 2005, celebrity chef Anthony Bourdain called it "the best restaurant in the world, period." For six years in a row, The French Laundry was awarded three Michelin stars, and Chef Thomas Keller and his team have received global accolades for their culinary creations. The restaurant has an enormous celebrity appeal too. On offer is a prix fixe menu, and the restaurant books six to eight months in advance.

French Laundry is also known for a wondrous, three-acre vegetable garden across the street that is, surprisingly, open to the public. This exceptionally bountiful garden supplies the restaurant, along with two local sister restaurants, Bouchon and Ad Hoc. At the entrance, you'll find a wooden stand with a map listing all the vegetables and their locations. Copies of the layout are available in the box under the stand for you to take and go exploring among the plants.

The vegetables grown here include more than 40 kinds of tomatoes and many varieties of beans, squashes, carrots, eggplant, peppers, potatoes, onions, beets, artichokes, cucumbers, spices, and even tiny cucamelons, also known as "mouse melons." The garden also hosts beehives, and the honey is served in the restaurant. There are chicken coops for Ameraucana hens. On the northwest side are two hoop houses, where the restaurant grows all its own starts, or seedlings. They source their seeds from Johnny's Selected Seeds and the Seed Savers Exchange.

So enjoy taking a stroll along the grass pads separating the 50 beds of flowers and vegetables, laid out in checkerboard pattern. The colors and smells change throughout the year. You can bring a sketch book or just relax and smell the flowers in bloom.

Address 6640 Washington Street, Yountville, CA 94599 | Getting there By car, from CA-29, take Madison Street in Yountville and turn right onto Washington Street. | Hours Daily 7am–9pm | Tip Take in a game of Bocce Ball at Yountville Park, just a short walk away (Washington Street at Madison Street, Yountville).

11 _The Grape Crusher Monument

A monument to vineyard workers

The Grape Crusher is a 6,000-pound, 15-foot-tall, bronze statue of a barefoot, 19th-century farm worker bent over a wine press. A monument to Napa Valley's life blood, the statue is a tribute to the vineyard workers and the whole wine industry of the region. The figure also represents the many anonymous migrant workers here. In fact, he is intended to be one of the "invisibles," the growing number of immigrants, both legal and illegal workers, who have powered the valley since Charles Krug first started it all in 1861.

The statue stands south of Napa on the crest of a coastal hill. He's a welcoming figure, who attracts wedding parties at sunset, and visitors can rest on benches and enjoy the spectacular views of this part of the county. He is very easy to see from Route 12 as you drive to Napa from Vallejo.

The sculpture was created by Gino Miles, a Santa Fe artist best known for his large, abstract pieces. He was first inspired by such European masters as Henry Moore and Constantin Brancusi. For this work, he used the lost wax process, known as *cire perdue*, and it took him 10 months to complete. The hollow statue, cast with 137 pieces welded together, was unveiled at Napa County's sesquicentennial celebration in 1988. This work is the largest sculpture cast west of the Mississippi.

And who are the actual crushers and pickers that cultivate the grapes for the approximately 2,500 grape growers in Napa and Sonoma County alone? Most of them are immigrants from Latin America, who came to Napa Valley in the 1940s and 50s through a temporary worker program that began in 1942. Today in Napa County, more than a quarter of all households are immigrant families. The majority come from Latin America originally, mostly Mexico.

Address Vista Point Park, Vista Point Drive, Napa, CA 94558 | **Getting there** By car, from CA-121/Napa Vallejo Highway, take Napa Valley Corporate Way, turn left onto Napa Valley Corporate Drive, and left on Vista Point Drive. | **Hours** Unrestricted | **Tip** Grape Culture is a winery that features wines produced with grapes from single vineyards with the intention of showcasing their unique growing conditions (2654 Napa Valley Corporate Drive, Napa, www.gcnapa.com).

12 Hog Island Oyster Company

In search of Sweetwater

In downtown Napa, across from the Napa Chef's Garden, is the Oxbow Public Market. It's a 40,000-square-foot hive of food bars, bakeries, cafés, and farm-fresh produce outlets. You can find some of the most venerable vendors in Northern California here in this one place, bound by a common trust in sustainable farming practices. One of those vendors is the Hog Island Oyster Company.

The Hog Island Oyster Company is a family-owned business that opened in 1983 and owns restaurants in San Francisco and the North Bay. Home base is in Marshall, a small town along Tomales Bay, where the company has a 160-acre intertidal farm. They also run the Boat Oyster Bar, an outdoor restaurant that offers fresh fish, clams, mussels, and Dungeness crab. The specialty of the house is black-shelled Pacific oysters, nicknamed sweetwaters, which are both salty and sweet at the same time. Their creamy clam chowder served with whole clams, and the grilled oysters with chipotle bourbon butter, are not to be missed.

Hog Island Oyster Company is especially interesting because it exemplifies the way some food companies are collaborating with scientific efforts. Hog Island works with The Nature Conservancy and the University of California at Santa Cruz to better understand the relationship between oyster aquaculture and the health of eelgrass beds. Hog Island is also allied with the University of California at Davis' Coastal and Marine Science Institute in monitoring acidification in Tomales Bay. The company is invested in sustainable farming as a Certified B Corporation shellfish farm committed to promoting positive changes in their community.

If you visit the venue in Marshall, you can join a variety of different tours. One tour explores the oyster farm and the nature of the oyster business. Another tour is more of a taster's treat.

Address 610 1st Street, Napa, CA 94559, +1 (707) 251-8113, www.hogislandoysters.com, obnapa@hogislandoysters.com | Getting there By car, from CA-29, take 1st Street in Napa to the destination. | Hours Mon–Fri 11:30am–8pm, Sat & Sun 11am–8pm | Tip Thirsty for a fresh cold beer? Visit craft brewery Fieldwork Brewing Company (1046 McKinstry Street, Napa, www.fieldworkbrewing.com).

13 Indian Springs
The hot springs' abundance

Along the eastern edge of the upper Napa County are the Maya-camas, a 50-mile-long, inner coastal mountain range that divides Napa and Sonoma Counties. For millennia, the area was home to several Native American tribes, notably the Wappo, who discovered a remarkable treasure in the local geology: mineral pools and steam, which they used for cooking and healing.

In the 1840s, this geothermal gold mine was named "The Geysers," which eventually led to the building of some 30 dry steam generating plants. More than 20 continue to operate and provide much of the electricity in half a dozen counties.

The Geysers also became a world-famous tourist destination. Among early speculators interested in the value of hot springs was Samuel Brannan, California's first millionaire. In 1862, he built a high-end resort in Calistoga called Indian Springs. It included a hotel and 13 cottages, a racetrack, observatory, skating rink, telegraph, bathhouse, and pool, as well as a winery and a cooperage shop. It was all a great success until a few years later, when Brannan lost the property in a divorce settlement.

Today, Indian Springs, California's oldest continuously operated geothermal pool and spa, is a 16-acre resort built on a quarter of the land Brannan used originally. It's a few blocks from the center of Calistoga and has the magical and nostalgic atmosphere of a 1930s movie studio backlot. The resort features bungalows and cottages, palm trees, flower and herb gardens, a spa, a bocce court, and two swimming pools, including an Olympic-sized pool built in 1913 and fed by on-site geysers, with temperatures from 85 to 102 degrees Fahrenheit. Amenities also include the Halotherapy Himalayan Salt Room.

The gardens and spa are open to the public, and you can purchase a day pass to the large pool. After your treatment, enjoy a meal at Sam's Social Club, also open to the public.

Address 1712 Lincoln Avenue, Calistoga, CA 94515, +1 (707) 709-8139,
www.indianspringscalistoga.com, reservations@indianspringscalistoga.com | Getting
there By car, from CA-29, take Lincoln Avenue in Calistoga to the destination. | Hours
Unrestricted | Tip For tasty sandwiches and more Brannan history, stop at Calistoga
Depot, the second-oldest train depot in California (1458 Lincoln Avenue, Calistoga,
www.calistogadepot.com).

14 La Cheve Mexican Bakery & Brews

Napa's oldest building

The oldest adobe building in the City of Napa stands on the corner of Soscol Avenue and Silverado Trail, a short drive from the historic mill area downtown. The building is now on the National Register of Historic Places and has a surprisingly contemporary quality. It was built in 1845 in the Spanish tradition, with adobe bricks made from horse manure, mud, and hay. This mixture was strong, especially compared to an earlier house made from the same materials that had collapsed.

Domitila Juarez Metcalf lived here for 80 years. She was one of the 11 children born to Maria and Don Cayetano Juarez, who built the structure as a family home. Cayetano was a powerful cattle rancher, a true Don, who incidentally gave the Tulocay Cemetery to the City of Napa, and he also funded the establishment of a mental health institute where the Napa State Hospital now stands. Domatila Juarez once described the terrible ways the house moved during the1906 earthquake. It rocked and shook, but in the end, there was nary a crack in a wall.

Today, the oldest building is a popular Mexican restaurant, bakery, and brewery named La Cheve, which opened in 2020 after an extensive renovation, using 1.5-foot-long bricks made with traditional methods. The process takes one day to make the bricks and then nearly a week for them to dry.

The restaurant is run by Cinthya Cisneros, who came to the US with her family from Mexico when she was four. The restaurant is a family affair, and the food is a celebration of their Mexican heritage. Popular items include tacos al pastor, ceviche, pastries made with different liqueurs, cronuts in flavors like mango and champagne, mimosa flights, and vegan and gluten-free pastries. They brew their own beer and bake their pastries daily.

Address 376 Soscol Avenue, Napa, CA 94559, +1 (707) 294-2142, www.ilovelacheve.com, ilovelacheve@gmail.com | Getting there By car, take CA-29 to CA-221 N to Soscol Avenue. | Hours Thu & Fri, Sun & Mon 7:30am–3pm, Sat 7:30am–4pm | Tip Walk through Moon Gate at China Point Overlook and enjoy the view of the Napa river at sunset (825 1st Street, Napa).

15 Litto's Hubcap Ranch

Folk art renaissance

Emanuel "Litto" Damonte, otherwise known as the Hubcap King of Pope Valley, was born in 1893 near Genoa on the Italian Riviera, in a small coastal town known for its quarries. In 1907, his father, a marble mason, was drawn to the US to work on the Memorial Church at Stanford University. Damonte the elder eventually brought his family to San Francisco and settled.

Meanwhile, Litto came of age after World War I. He found work as a tile setter and a cement contractor, got married, and had 10 children. In 1941, he bought a ranch in Pope Valley, just west of Lake Berryessa, where an odd creative opportunity came his way. The road that ran past his property had several potholes, one of which became known as the "wheel-eating pothole" and delivered an endless harvest of runaway hubcaps. In fact, between 1955 and 1985, when Litto died, he had collected thousands of hubcaps – as many as 5,000 by one estimate. There were so many that he felt inspired to hang them around his property – on fences and trees, on buildings in his courtyard, shed doors, on the garage, and on curbs. He added chains fashioned from aluminum soda and beer pop-tops. Passersby often get the sense that it's a folk art installation, but Litto was merely a dutiful collector with an eye for the odd.

Pope Valley, population fewer than 600, has a grocery store; the remains of an iron works factory; a junkyard filled with old Cadillacs, trucks and tractors; and the Pope Valley Winery. Today, if the gate is open, you can walk into Litto's front yard and talk with his own children or grandchildren. They still marvel at the whimsy of it all. Yet perhaps the most unexpected quality of the place is how quiet it all is.

In May 1981, Damonte's property was named a California State Registered Landmark. Litto Damonte's grandson maintains this art environment, and he even adds new elements of his own.

Address 6654 Pope Valley Road, Pope Valley, CA 94567 | Getting there By car, from CA-29, take Deer Park Road to Howell Mountain Road and then turn left onto Pope Valley Road. | Hours Viewable from outside only unless the gate is open | Tip Family-owned Pope Valley Winery just across the way offers tours and tastings (6613 Pope Valley Road, www.popevalleywinery.com).

16 Monticello Dam
A spillway of history

In 1878, the town of Monticello was thriving, with two hotels, a general store, and a post office. It was a wealthy place anchored by 12,000 acres of farmland along Putah Creek in the Berryessa Valley, named after the Mexican family that originally owned it. In 1880, a rancher built a three-story, 22 room mansion here. In the early 1900s, the Monticello Municipal Band played Sunday afternoon concerts, and the Monticello rodeo was the biggest attraction in Napa County. Then the economy crashed in 1929.

The idea of damming up Berryessa Valley circulated in the 1930s and grew popular after World War II, particularly in nearby Solano county. Still, opposition in Monticello was firm. Among those who defended saving Monticello was Dorothea Lang, the great photographer, who captured the town in a series of spreads in *Aperture* magazine. On the other side, Governor Earl Warren argued that a dam was the only way to counter inevitable water shortages. Eventually, pro-dam interests prevailed, and the commercial district, homes, school, and church were all removed, except for some stone steps. Trees, grape vines, and fences were cut to six inches. The dam was completed in 1957.

These days, Lake Berryessa serves farmers in Solano county and consumers in Vallejo, along with boat owners, hikers, and the café trade. You can see the effect of the relentless fires in recent years. The view of the lake itself is more dramatic than beautiful.

At the southern end of the dam, at Devil's Gate, there is a large cement drain known as the Morning Glory spillway or simply, the "glory hole," designed to channel overflows down and around the bottom of the dam. It looks like a cooling tower in a reactor. The tower, 72 feet across, the largest drain of its kind, hasn't served its purpose since 2019 because of drought, but when there is enough water to drain, the sight is mesmerizing.

Address East End of Lake Berryessa, Napa, CA 94558, www.usbr.gov/projects | Getting there By car, from I-80, take exit onto Lagoon Valley Road and then left onto Cherry Glen Road. Turn left onto Pleasant Valley Road for 13 miles, then left onto CA-128, and continue 4.5 miles to the dam. | Hours Unrestricted | Tip Just prior to its inundation by Lake Berryessa, the Monticello Cemetery was relocated to the community of Spanish Flat near the western shore of the lake (4380 Berryessa Knoxville Road).

17 Mt. Saint Helena
"Human mountain"

It was the Wappo people who originally referred to Mt. Saint Helena as *Kanamota*, or "Human Mountain." Then the Spanish arrived and renamed it Mt. Mayacamas. Finally, in 1841, Russian surveyors out of Fort Ross proclaimed it Princess Helena de Gagarin after the wife of Alexander Rotchev, the fort's Russian commander. This magnificent mountain includes five peaks – the tallest is around 4,400 feet – spread over Lake County to the north, Sonoma, and Napa. The whole area is a geological wonderland filled with domes, cones, and 2.4-million-year-old volcanic rocks from the Clear Lake Volcanic Field.

The best way to experience Mt. Saint Helena is to hike it. There are many trails of varying difficulty. Considering how quickly parking lots fill up, seasoned visitors arrive around 7am, particularly on weekends. One of the most popular trails is the Robert Louis Stevenson Memorial Trail, named after the famed Scottish novelist. The hike is barely one mile from the trailhead to the main monument, which is a large bronze book, marking the site of the Stevenson cabin that stood here once but is now long gone. Stevenson wrote about the summer of 1880 in his book *The Silverado Squatters*, when he and his wife Fanny camped out on their honeymoon near an old mine.

The trail is narrow and winds through evergreen forests on the north side of the mountain and past chaparral to the south. There are occasional rocky patches. The going gradually changes from easy to difficult. The challenge here is patience. From the bronze book, it's another four miles to Mt. Saint Helena's peak, where, on a clear day, you can see Sonoma County all the way to the Pacific Ocean, as well as Napa Valley, Lake County to the north, Mt. Diablo on the east side of the bay, and majestic snow-capped Mt. Shasta. The views are truly breathtaking. The round-trip total distance is 10 miles and takes four to six hours.

Address Mt. Saint Helena Trailhead, 4625 Lake County Highway, Calistoga, www.alltrails.com/trail/us/california/mount-saint-helena-trail--2 | Getting there By car, from CA-29, take Lincoln Avenue in Calistoga and continue onto Lake County Road to the destination. | Hours Daily dawn–dusk | Tip Visit the Santa Helena Historical Society to find out about the area's rich history (1255 Oak Avenue, Saint Helena, www.shstory.org).

18 Napa River

The river in recovery

The Napa River begins in the Mayacamas Mountains just below the summit of Mt. Saint Helena in Robert Louis Stevenson State Park. It then drops down into Napa Valley above Calistoga, running south past Saint Helena and Oakville, to the city of Napa, its head of navigation, or the highest point ships can reach in the river. Below Napa, the river forms a tidal estuary as it enters San Pablo Bay at Vallejo.

The river is 55 miles long and a shadow of its original self, though certainly not the terrible torrent it was in 1986. That flood was the worst the city had ever seen. Three people died, and more than 250 houses were destroyed. These days, the river is calm and still suffers the lingering effects of decades of damming and pollution.

In recent years, local communities and vineyards along the river have joined together in the Rutherford Restoration Project. The effort has been to bring back the coho salmon and steelhead trout, and there's been some success. Beavers have also reappeared. If you drive along Soscol Avenue in downtown Napa, you can see a beaver lodge on Tulucay Creek at Soscol Avenue.

Among the ways to experience the river are kayaking and rafting trips north of Napa, or ocean kayaking and motorboating to the south. The river is also a birder's paradise. Look for green-winged teals, mergansers, mallards, and wood ducks, along with the endangered clapper rail. Other animals along the river include river otters, gray foxes, and bobcats. Occasionally, harbor porpoises venture up the tidal portion of the river all the way to downtown Napa!

There are numerous trails to hike and revel in the beauty of the river. However, if you're after a bit of romance, take a very special ride in an authentic Venetian gondola with a skilled gondolier. You'll find the boat moored at a wharf at the bottom of Main Street in front of the Waterfront Grill.

Address Napa County, www.visitnapavalley.com/blog/post/enjoy-napa-river | Getting there Varies by location | Hours Unrestricted | Tip Angèle Restaurant and Bar located in the old boat house on the tip of the Riverfront offers delicious French fare (540 Main Street, Napa, www.angelerestaurant.com).

19 Native American Garden
The weaves of Laura Fish Somersal

A few years before she died, Laura Fish Somersal organized an herb garden in Bothe-Napa Valley State Park, which lies between Saint Helena and Calistoga. It's classified as an "ethnic botanical garden," partly because Somersal, who died in 1990, was a Mihilakawna Pomo and a Geyserville Wappo. She was an internationally recognized weaver, whose baskets display an extraordinary variety of designs and functions – and enormous beauty. Indeed, she is often regarded as the last Wappo weaver. She was also a Native American cultural consultant and lecturer, and a language scholar.

Fish's garden, which is set on three-quarters of an acre next to the visitor's entrance to the Bothe Park, is a Native American medicine chest filled with trees and plants, many holding unique qualities and often still used today. You'll find ghost pines, or gray pines, known for their nuts, especially good for roasting. The roots were used to weave large-twined baskets, and pitch from the ghost pine serves as a chewing gum. Also look for the California black oak – its acorns were regarded as "the staff of life" among the Wappo and Patwin people.

Other garden highlights include sedge, Pacific rush, wild tobacco, hazelnut, redbud (its bark served as a twine), and even poison oak, which has been used as a stain for bullrush roots in basketry. In the garden, you'll also see sandbar willows, yerba santa, toyon trees, blue elderberry, California bay laurel, of course, and buckeye nuts, those shiny, brown orbs sometimes used in place of acorns. Interestingly, buckeye nuts are poisonous when eaten raw and were used in lakes and streams to stun fish.

The garden was blessed by elders initially and remains a sacred resource for Native Americans. It has always been used for ceremonial occasions. You can walk through the garden and into the park's trail system.

Address 3801 Saint Helena Highway N, Calistoga, CA 94515, +1 (707) 942-4575, www.napaoutdoors.org/parks/bothe-napa-valley-state-park | Getting there By car, take CA-29 N four miles past Saint Helena. The destination will be on the left. | Hours Daily 8am−dusk | Tip Visit Clos Pegase Winery for its 1980s postmodernist architecture (1060 Dunaweal Lane, Calistoga, www.clospegase.com).

20 The Petrified Forest
From redwood to gray stone

In his exquisite traveler's tale *The Silverado Squatters*, Robert Louis Stevenson recounts the first time he visited the Petrified Forest, which straddles the road between Santa Rosa and Calistoga. It was 1880, and the place was already an attraction for both tourists and scientists. Stevenson and his wife Fanny stopped by for a chat with the proprietor Charles Evans, known as "Petrified Charlie," who became a close friend of theirs.

In *The Silverado Squatters*, Fanny asks who found the forest. "'I was that man,' replied Evans. 'I was cleaning up the pastures when I found this' – kicking a great redwood seven feet in diameter that lay there on its side, hollow heart, clinging lumps of bark, all changed into gray stone, with veins of quartz between what had been the layers of wood."

Evans goes on to explain the process of petrification: how this redwood forest, with some pines and oaks, had been buried for more than three million years in volcanic ash from the nearby volcano, Mt. Saint Helena; how hundreds of feet of ash prevented bacteria from forming that would allow the trees to rot; and how mineral-rich ground water seeped through the layers of ash and then evaporated, leaving the minerals to seep into the pores of the wood. In sum, it was a process of permineralization and replacement that created these three-dimensional fossils.

Petrified Charlie discovered the forest in 1870. It soon drew the interest of a renowned paleontologist from Yale named Othniel Charles Marsh and an equally renowned paleobotanist from UC Berkeley, Ralph Chaney. The two universities continue to collaborate in studying the site today. In 1914, Ollie Bockee purchased the land to create a site encouraging scientific discovery, preservation, and education, and her family still owns the property. There are two half-mile trails to explore this wondrous and eerie forest.

Address 4100 Petrified Forest Road, Calistoga, CA 94515, +1 (707) 942-6667, www.petrifiedforest.org, www.petrifiedforest.org, pforest@sonic.net | **Getting there** By car, from CA-29, take Petrified Forest Road in Calistoga to the destination. | **Hours** Daily 9am–5pm | **Tip** Lovina serves delicious modern American cuisine (1107 Cedar Street, Calistoga, www.lovinacalistoga.com).

21_The Pfeiffer Building
The nefarious lives of Napa's oldest building

The area of Napa known as Spanishtown has slipped out of history. No statues mark its passing. But in its heyday, the place was raucous and occasionally murderous, diverse, and largely poor. It was home to Spanish, Chinese, and Italian immigrants. It also hosted a red-light district along Clinton Street. The Pfeiffer Building, a narrow two-story, red brick structure with an architectural design from the Italianate period, rose up in Spanishtown in 1875, and it's one of the oldest buildings in Napa. Throughout its history, it has been a brewery, a Chinese laundry, and a boarding house.

The Pfeiffer Building was initially the Pfeiffer/Barth Brewery and then became The Stone Saloon a decade later. Upstairs, there was an upscale bordello run by May Howard, remembered as a pleasant-looking, well-dressed matron, who paid her bills on time and was well respected. Clients gathered at the back door and were carefully screened and bounced back outside as necessary. Tricks cost $3. Policemen were welcomed, which reflected a culture in which prostitution was seen as a social necessity.

Spanishtown was also the site of the last public hanging in California in 1897, after the horrible murder of Mrs. Greenwood, a farmer's wife. The judge was so disgusted by the crime that at sentencing, he ordered the perpetrator to be hanged in the Napa County Jail Yard.

For the last 20 years, the Pfeiffer Building has been The Vintner's Collective, a space for Napa boutique wineries that don't have tasting quarters of their own. It's become a popular spot for aficionados and for curious passersby alike. The centerpiece here is a long testing bar counter. Upstairs is a vintner's room for the private tastings, available by appointment. As an homage to the historic and once thriving red light district, a single red light is suspended from above the stairway leading to the second floor.

Address 1245 Main Street, Napa, CA 94559, www.vintnerscollective.com | **Getting there** By car, from CA-29/Soscol Avenue, take Clinton Street in Napa to the destination. | **Hours** Daily 11am–7pm | **Tip** For a tasty lunch or dinner, visit the Napa Valley Bistro across the street (975 Clinton Street, Napa, www.napavalleybistro.com).

22 Quixote Winery
The world according to Hundertwasser

Several miles north of Napa in the foothills between two other vineyards, you'll find Quixote, a well-regarded boutique winery. It's set on 42 acres and is best known for petite syrahs. It may be even better known for the manor house winery, a long, low, wavy structure with olive trees, bushes, and grass growing on the roof, as well as its golden onion dome and brightly colored ceramic tiles. These tiles are reminiscent of Mondrian's squares, but without any right angles. None at all. The aesthetic here is organic not geometric. Look quickly, and you may notice the quirky spirit of Gaudí.

It's all from the whimsical minds of Carl Doumani, Quixote's founder, and his close friend, the Viennese artist, sculptor, free thinker, and architect Friedensreich Hundertwasser (1928–2000), commissioned by Doumani to design the house. It took 10 years to complete and opened in 2007. Hundertwasser did just one project in the US, and it was this winery and grounds, and certain bottle labels. He also persuaded Doumani to grow organic grapes.

Note that every window in the house has slightly different dimensions, and the floors are deliberately uneven as an appeal to one's sense of balance in the natural world. "A melody to the feet," as Hundertwasser once put it. In artistic terms, the Quixote winery stands in protest against dark, humorless henges that suggest the tyranny of the straight line and a grid-like world made solely with machine tolerances.

Such was the rebellion of Hundertwasser, a man who insisted on his personal freedom, lectured in the nude, lived for several years on an old wooden freighter, and, according to a 2007 *New York Times* article, once "lived on mush made from 100-pound sacks of wheat." As for his works, his most famous – and controversial – is the 1986 Hundertwasserhaus, a colorful apartment building in Vienna, the city where he grew up.

Address 6126 Silverado Trail, Napa, CA 94558, +1 (707) 944-2659, www.quixotewinery.com, info@quixotewinery.com | Getting there By car, from CA-29, take Yountville Cross Road and then turn right onto Silverado Trail. | Hours Daily 10am–3pm by appointment | Tip Rector Reservoir Wildlife Area Trailhead just north of the winery offers great hikes and bird watching (near 7292 Silverado Trail, Napa, www.alltrails.com/trail/us/california).

23 Robert Louis Stevenson Museum

Ode to the Scottish author

Visitors might be surprised to find the Robert Louis Stevenson Museum, originally known as the Silverado Museum, a block off Main Street in Saint Helena. Perhaps more surprising to some, this modest, one-room affair next to the town library is among the world's most distinguished museums dedicated to the writer.

Stevenson, a slender and pale Scottish novelist and poet, was a Napa Valley presence in the summer of 1880, while on honeymoon with his bohemian wife Fanny and her son from her previous marriage. Stevenson's health was fragile due to bronchial congestion, and he hoped that the dry air of Napa would help his condition. For a time, they lived at an abandoned old mining camp up on Mt. Saint Helena, where he wrote *The Silverado Squatters* (1883), a travel memoir about life in Napa Valley.

The museum opened in 1969 and contains some 9,000 items related to the writer, including letters, manuscripts, journals, rare periodicals, paintings, sculptures, photographs, scrapbooks, childhood letters, and drawings. Only a fraction of the material is on display at any one time and continuously in rotation. It's worth noting that in the last century, critics have elevated Stevenson's place in the pantheon of English-language writers from an author of children's books to the ranks of Joseph Conrad.

Other items of "Stevensoniana" include the last words he ever wrote; pages from *The Strange Case of Dr. Jekyll and Mr. Hyde*; Stevenson's personal copy of his first book, *An Inland Voyage*; the copy of *A Child's Garden of Verses* that he presented to his wife Fanny; unpublished poems; and more than a hundred books from his personal library in Samoa. Among the most personal items here are the desk at which he wrote *Treasure Island*, and his wedding ring.

Address 1490 Library Lane, Saint Helena, CA 94754, +1 (707) 963-3757, www.stevensonmuseum.org, info@stevensonmuseum.org | Getting there By car, from CA-29, take Adams Street in Calistoga and then turn left onto Library Lane. | Hours Tue–Sat noon–4pm | Tip Look for the two welcome signs in Napa Valley featuring Stevenson's famous quote, "… and the wine is bottled poetry" (along CA-29 and 7647 Saint Helena Highway, Napa).

24 Sharpsteen Museum

History of a 19th-century small town

Ben Sharpsteen (1895–1980) was the great Walt Disney animator and film director who dominated the genre for nearly half a century. He won a record 11 Oscars and is best known for his animated feature films, including *Pinocchio*, *Fantasia*, *Dumbo*, and *Cinderella*. He's also revered for his documentary series, notably *The Living Desert*. In 1962, he retired to Calistoga where, in 1978, he established the Sharpsteen Museum. The museum exhibits a trove of memorabilia from the town's beginnings, as well as objects from the tragic journey of the Donner-Reed Party, such as the cast-iron cooking pot the families used while they were stranded in the Sierras.

The museum's centerpiece is a 30-foot-long diorama built by Sharpsteen and his Disney colleagues. It captures the original Brannan Springs grounds during the period from 1862 to 1868. "This is not simply a collection of miniaturized structures," the museum's director Kathy Bazzoli will tell you. "There are men, women, children, dogs, cats, horses, and landscaping throughout. All the people are wearing clothing from that era. All have different faces. Not one figure is static – all are in movement."

The museum also captures the life and times of Samuel Brannan, who founded Calistoga in 1859. Brannan was a Mormon and a controversial character in church circles. At 33, he was California's first millionaire, making an early fortune selling mining supplies. He owned a newspaper chain that he used to guide prospectors to gold rush strikes and attract investors to his projects. He built a train that once ran from Napa to Calistoga, an extension from the line connected to the steamer dock in Vallejo. Brannan opened a dairy, a winery, a brandy distillery, and Indian Hot Springs.

Attached to the museum is the original and restored Sam Brannan Cottage, where Robert Louis Stevenson and his wife Fanny stayed in 1880.

Address 1311 Washington Street, Calistoga, CA 94515, +1 (707) 942-5911, www.sharpsteenmuseum.org, info@sharpsteenmuseum.org | Getting there By car, from CA-29, take Lincoln Avenue in Calistoga and then turn left onto Washington Street. | Hours Mon–Fri noon–3pm, Sat & Sun noon–4pm | Tip Solbar, the restaurant and bar at the Solage resort, offers a variety of amazing libations (755 Silverado Trail, Calistoga, www.aubergeresorts.com/solage/dine/solbar).

25__Veterans Home History Case

A museum finds a home among the truly brave

On the grounds of the Veterans Home of California in Yountville is the Napa Valley Museum. As a Blue Star Museum, it welcomes active duty military and their families for free during the summer.

Look for the Veterans Home History Case, where you'll see the Congressional Medal of Honor awarded to Colonel Nelson Holderman (1885–1953) for his bravery with the Lost Battalion during World War I. Holderman was commandant of the Veterans Home in Yountville for 30 years. The museum also features world-class rotating exhibitions of artifacts from the Veterans Home's own collection. The Spotlight Gallery presents work by local and regional artists, and the History Gallery shares the culture of Napa County.

The Veterans Home was first created in 1884 to care for the survivors of the Mexican American War (1846–1848) and the American Civil War (1861–1865). Covering 960 acres, this institution is the largest veterans' home in the US, and offers residential housing, along with recreational, social, and therapeutic activities. These days, there are some 1,200 aging or disabled warriors. They represent World War II (1939–1945), the Korean War (1950–1953), the Vietnam War (1955–1975), Operation Desert Storm (1991–1991), and Operation Enduring Freedom (2001–2014).

The heart of the Veterans Home was once the multi-faith Armistice Chapel, built in late 1918. The architecture is described as "simple English country Gothic." In addition to services, the chapel was used for choral and theatrical performances, and also for the funeral services of residents and employees. In 1959, it was decommissioned and fell into disuse. It remains closed, although tours pass by it. But it is still a monument to the founding spirit of the home, which was always about finding purpose in life and the value of good work after military service.

Address 55 Presidents Circle, Yountville, CA 94599, +1 (707) 944-0500, www.napavalleymuseum.org | **Getting there** By car, from CA-2, take the exit toward Yountville/Veterans Home onto California Drive, then turn right onto President's Circle. | **Hours** Wed–Sun 10am–4pm | **Tip** Hungry for classic French cuisine? Visit Bistro Jeanty (6510 Washington Street, Yountville, www.bistrojeanty.com).

26 Villa Ca'toga
Marchiori's villa favolosa

Carlo Marchiori was born in 1937 in Bassano del Grappa, a small town west of Venice, best known for Andrea Palladio's Ponte Vecchio, designed in 1569. Carlo's mother imagined and hoped that he might become a priest or even a bureaucrat. He preferred to be an artist and set off for Padua to learn various crafts. He went on to live in Canada and became a book illustrator. He also made animated films, one of which was nominated for an Academy Award.

In 1956, he made his way to the US. He became famous for the frescoes and murals he created for hotels such as the Bellagio in Las Vegas. In 1987, he bought five acres outside Calistoga and began building a villa, which he called Ca'Toga Galleria d'Arte. It's at once a studio, gallery, retreat, and his home.

There are various houses in Sonoma and Napa that are highly creative in some unexpected way, but Ca'Toga may be the most compelling of the lot – more whimsical, more theatrical. Altogether, it's a compendium of acquired knowledge and taste, combining styles and references, including Veronese, Venetian, and Palladian architecture. The villa is surrounded by Greco-Roman ruins, Thai *stupas*, a Roman pool, a life-sized alligator, and a Doric temple. Marchiori fashioned it all himself, making each piece by hand, including cement rock features, as well as furniture, ceramics, and columns.

You can take a guided tour to see the Villa's lavish interior. It begins with a main salon, followed by several large rooms: a Pompeian Room, the Library, a Greek Room, and a Birdcage Room designed to give the viewer the sensation of being a bird. There's also a Cow Room and a Native American Room. Some murals were painted on large canvas strips and then attached to the walls. Others were painted directly onto the walls. The total effect is that of an anthropology museum, where you travel from one state of mind to another.

Address 3061 Myrtledale Road, Calistoga, CA 94515, +1 (707) 942-0212, www.catoga.com, info@catoga.com | Getting there By car, from CA-29, take Tubbs Lane in Calistoga and then turn right onto Myrtledale Road. | Hours Tours Sat 11am by appointment only | Tip In downtown Calistoga, you'll find Ca'Toga Art Gallery, a showcase of Carlo Marchiori's art (1206 Cedar Street, Calistoga, www.catoga.com).

27 ___ Water Towers
An architectural idiom

Water towers, or tank houses, first appeared on Northern California farms and in towns in the 1850s. According to some scholars of architectural idioms, they may have been first built in Mendocino County in 1857. Today, despite their dwindling number, you can still see them along rural roads in Napa and Sonoma.

Look for a classic example of California water towers at Silver Oak Cellars in Oakville. The winery is well known for its Cabernet Sauvignon, and its iconic water tower highlights its wine labels. The tall, white tower is visible from the road and stands apart from the building, just outside the tasting room. It's the only building that was untouched by a 2006 fire that destroyed all the other structures. Among the lost buildings was the original dairy barn.

Water towers, typically three stories high and with tapered walls, were often hidden behind redwood siding for aesthetic reasons. The tanks themselves were also made from redwood trees because the wood didn't rot. The first iterations were set over hand-dug wells not more than 50 feet deep. They were often built next to a main house because their purpose was to provide water for the home and the garden, but not the barnyard and crops. These became known as "domestic tank houses."

There are half a dozen water towers in and around Bennett Valley, the premium vineyard area just east of Santa Rosa. You can also find tank houses by Old Redwood Highway, Petaluma Hill Road, and Railroad Avenue in Penngrove. Some water towers stand in ruin, although their true condition is not always apparent as you drive by. Others are empty, and still others have been transformed into fashionable living spaces, with elaborate staircases. Although a precursor of today's green technologies, water towers became obsolete in the 1930s with the advent of electric pumps, water mains, and declining water tables.

Address 915 Oakville Cross Road, Oakville, CA 94562, www.silveroak.com | Getting there By car, from CA-29, take Oakville Cross Road just north of Yountville. | Hours Unrestricted | Tip You can see another historic but more industrial water tower at Martin Ray Vineyards (2191 Laguna Road, Santa Rosa, www.martinraywinery.com).

28 Armstrong Redwoods SNR
A portal to the "wood wide web"

Colonel James Armstrong was 50 years old when he arrived in Guerneville in 1874. Born in Waynesville, Ohio, Armstrong would become a journalist, a surveyor, and a Union Army officer. He was captured during the Civil War and made a dramatic escape. He moved to Sonoma in 1874, where he got into the lumber business, opened a sawmill, and became a local real estate developer, offering homes at low cost.

Armstrong fell in love with old-growth redwoods, gave up cutting, and became a renowned conservationist. He had purchased a grove of redwoods, and in 1878 he gifted 440 acres of forest to his daughter Kate. The park's website states that he listed value as "one dollar, love and affection." He added more acres over time and gradually set up a series of protections through his daughters that eventually became a state-owned natural reserve.

Now covering 805 acres, Armstrong Redwoods State Natural Reserve (SNR) has a wet and mild climate that offers a perfect setting for coastal redwoods to thrive. Beyond the redwoods, you'll also find a mix of Douglas fir, Pacific madrones, bay laurel, and tanoak. The oldest tree is a 1,400-years-old redwood named after Armstrong. The tallest tree is longer than a football field. The forest is a refuge for endangered animals, such as mountain lions, coho salmon, and the marbled murrelet, a seabird that nests only at the top of redwoods. The top of these trees collect mats of soil, which support another world of plants and animals, as do their roots.

The reserve brings to mind the 2021 book by the ecologist Suzanne Simard, *Finding the Mother Tree: Discovering the Wisdom of the Forest*. She explores the way trees communicate over vast networks, warning and even arguing with each other. "It's enough to take a deep breath," writes Simard, "and contemplate the social network of the forest and how this is critical for evolution."

Address 17000 Armstrong Woods Road, Guerneville, CA 95446, +1 (707) 869-2015, www.parks.ca.gov | Getting there By car, from US-101, take exit 494 onto River Road, continue 15 miles, then turn right onto Armstrong Woods Road. | Hours Daily 8am–dusk | Tip Stay overnight at Fern Grove Cottages in Guerneville, many of which have fireplaces and free bicycles (16650 River Road, Guerneville, www.dawnranch.com/stay/#grove).

29 Bartholomew Park
The strange life of Agoston Haraszthy

Bartholomew Park is well known to locals for a three-mile hike, along a narrow path that rises and falls. It may be arduous for some. But rest assured that there are benches, steps, occasional shade, and gratifying views of the valley all along the route. The park, named after Frank and Antonia Bartholomew, who purchased the land in 1943, is 375 acres of mostly oak woodlands and chaparral, and also, in one part, redwoods and Douglas firs. You come to the park for the walk, but also for the history, which crackles with ambition, eccentricity, very good fortune, and very bad luck. Then add a "castle" that burned down, a suspected murder, and several ghosts.

The park's modern history revolves mostly around a sprightly Hungarian count named Agoston Haraszthy. He arrived on the scene around 1857. He was the consummate entrepreneur, known as the "father of California viticulture," and he built the Buena Vista winery, as well as a fabulous Palladian style villa, which burned down and has been replaced by an architectural replica, now a historic landmark.

In the early 1900s, one of the wineries in the park was converted into a home for wayward women from the streets of San Francisco. The story goes that during an earthquake retrofit in the 1970s, the body of one of the women was found in a basement wall.

But of all the characters connected to the park, Agoston Haraszthy is the most colorful. He was not only a world-famous vintner, but he also ran the first commercial steamboat on the upper Mississippi. He was the first sheriff of San Diego. He lost everything at one time due to a recession and poor judgment in managing his vineyard. Two of his sons married two of General Mariano Vallejo's daughters. In 1868, he bought property in Nicaragua to start a sugar business. One day he disappeared, possibly after falling into a river filled with alligators.

Address 1695 Castle Road, Sonoma, CA 95476, +1 (707) 938-2244,
www.bartholomewpark.org | Getting there By car, from CA-121 take 8th Street E, then
turn left onto E Napa Street, right onto 7th Street East, and right onto Castle Road. |
Hours Daily 10am–6pm | Tip Stop for a glass of wine at nearby Bartholomew Winery
within the park's boundaries (1000 Vineyard Lane, Sonoma, www.bartholomewestate.com).

30 Bear Flag Monument

The bear and the star are born

In the Sonoma Plaza you first encounter a sculpture of a seated General Mariano Vallejo, and then a monument to the Bear Flag Revolt. It was Mariano Vallejo who laid out the streets of Sonoma. He was a renaissance figure: Spanish by birth, a general and statesman, a very wealthy landowner, a California patrician, and, finally, a historian. He wrote the "true history" of California, in which he included that remarkable scene one morning of June 1846, when a scruffy militia appeared outside his door at Casa Grande.

That day was the opening of the three-week-long Bear Flag Revolt against California's Mexican government. It was not entirely bloodless. Vallejo invited the rebel leaders into his home, while a next-door neighbor brought over a barrel of brandy. This effort didn't keep Vallejo from being briefly imprisoned in his own home by American frontiersmen. But neither did he lose his conviction in always finding reconciliation between victor and vanquished.

The Bear Flag Revolt took place during June and July 1846, when a group of American settlers decided to declare California an independent republic and raised their flag in Sonoma. The flag featured the stripe, the star, and the bear. The Revolt lasted less than a month.

After that, the flag was given to teenager John Elliott Montgomery, who wrote to his mother, "Their Flag consisted of a Star Union with a Grizzly bear in the center looking up at the star and under the Bear the words 'Republic of California' on the lower border there was a red Stripe of Flannel the whole was composed of a piece of white cotton & Blackberry juice there being no paint in the country. I have the original & only Flag of the California Republic in my possession & esteem it quite a prize." Montgomery disappeared in 1846 while headed to Sutter's Fort. In 1911, the Bear Flag was established as the official flag of California.

Address Sonoma Plaza, 453 1st Street E, Sonoma, CA 95476 | Getting there By car, take CA-12/Broadway to E Napa Street in Sonoma. | Hours Unrestricted | Tip Take a Sonoma wine country tour on a three-wheeled electric trike with Pushpak Motors (414 1st Street E, Sonoma, www.pushpakmotors.net).

31 Beltane Ranch

Home of Mary Ellen Pleasant, millionaire

Mary Ellen Pleasant (1814–1904) was an abolitionist, an entrepreneur, and likely one of the first Black millionaires. She is largely unknown in part because so much of her life remains a mystery or is disputed, but think of her along with Rosa Parks and Harriet Tubman. She had close ties to Nantucket Island. She arrived in San Francisco from the East Coast in 1852 and spent most of her adult life there. Although she brought gold coins of her own, apparently close to $500,000 in today's value, she began working as a housekeeper in wealthy homes, where she would pick up investment tips. On a census form in 1890, she identified herself as a "capitalist by profession."

She was also a liberal activist and philanthropist. She worked on the Underground Railroad in San Francisco, she supported the local Black press, along with the Athenaeum Building, a library, and a Black community center. Much like Rosa Parks, she once sued a streetcar company when a trolley wouldn't pick her up, even though there were plenty of seats and she had a ticket. The case went to the California Supreme Court, which ruled in her favor. Her political influence may also have helped overturn a law banning Black testimony in California courts.

In the late 1800s, Pleasant purchased the Beltane Ranch in Glen Ellen – 2,000 acres including vineyard and five homesteads – as her vacation home. She designed the main house, inspired by New Orleans' Southern plantation-style architecture. Interestingly, all the staircases are on the outside. Recognized as a Black Historical Site, the pale yellow Beltane Ranch, now a bed-and-breakfast inn, remains much the same today.

You'll find Pleasant's grave in the Tulocay Cemetery in Napa. The gravestone is a small, black, metal sculpture with the inscription, *Mary Ellen Pleasant, Mother of Civil Rights in California, 1817–1904. "She was a friend of John Brown."*

Address 11775 Sonoma Highway, Glen Ellen, CA 95442, +1 (707) 833-4233, www.beltaneranch.com | Getting there By car, take CA-12 to Foster Road about eight miles north of Sonoma. | Hours By appointment only | Tip Hike to the seasonal waterfall nestled in Sugarloaf Ridge State Park. From the summit of Bald Mountain, you can see the Golden Gate Bridge (2605 Adobe Canyon Road, Kenwood, www.parks.ca.gov).

32 Bodega Head

The place to watch migrating gray whales

Driving west from Santa Rosa down the Bodega Highway, you'll come to Bodega, a village of 200. It's forever known for the scene in Hitchcock's 1963 film, *The Birds*. A few minutes later, you'll come to Highway 1, where you'll turn right and reach Bodega Bay, a fishing town made up of crab diners, inns, galleries, and 1,100 people. Some scenes in *The Birds* were shot here as well.

The geography below the town includes a long, narrow bay with a harbor formed by a four-mile-long peninsula, with a flat surface and marked by high bluffs, like a slice of brie. The southern tip of the peninsula is called Bodega Head.

Follow a mile-long hiking trail on Bodega Head, and you will arrive at a spectacular site for spotting whales. This natural wonder goes from late December to mid-May, when approximately 20,000 eastern gray whales glide north to Alaska. In the fall, they return south to their breeding grounds off Baja California. The round-trip is 12,000 miles. Gray whales can reach a length of 50 feet, weigh 90,000 pounds, and live to the age of 80. In some places, they're known as "devil fish" due to their firm resistance to being hunted. Here, though, they're known as "friendly ones" because of their curiosity about those who come out in boats to look at them.

The peninsula and Bodega Head lie on the Pacific Tectonic Plate, while the town of Bodega Bay lies on the North American Plate. The dividing line is the 750-mile-long San Andreas Fault, running from Southern California on and off the coast through Bodega Bay and up to Cape Mendocino. The fault's shaking motion is "right-lateral strike-slip." The area is filled with "sister faults." What a perfect place to build a nuclear power plant! That was the plan in the early 1960s. But after a long, vicious battle, the plan was quashed. One positive result, though, was that long-term coastal protections were established.

Address Westshore Road, Bodega Bay, CA 94923, www.parks.ca.gov | Getting there By car, from US-101, take exit 488B to CA-12 for 17 miles, then turn right onto CA-1 and then left onto Eastshore Road in Bodega Bay. Turn right onto Bay Flat Road, which becomes Westshore Road. Continue to the parking lot at the trailhead on the Pacific Ocean side of the peninsula. | Hours Unrestricted | Tip Annello Family Crab and Seafood is a perfect place to stop for Dungeness crab after a windy hike (1820 Westshore Road, Bodega Bay, www.anellofamilyseafood.com).

33 Bodega Marine Reserve

The Pacific Ocean at your feet

Bodega Bay is a quaint fishing village with a harbor and a bay. Across from this village, on the other side of the bay, there's a four-mile-long peninsula, which is the Bodega Marine Reserve, a remote and rocky kind of place, where you brave the bluster to watch sea lions, gray whales, killer whales, and white sharks ply the ocean in front of you.

On the ocean side of the peninsula, above Horseshoe Cove, is the UC Davis Marine Laboratory, one of several UC facilities along the California coast. This has been a research area since the 1920s. The full-time lab opened in 1966 and includes classrooms, lecture halls, libraries, and computer facilities, as well as an aquarium, some of which are open to visitors. Educating the public about various marine issues, particularly climate change, is part of the lab's charter.

On weekly tours, student docents, who are particularly well versed, introduce you to complex marine ecosystems involving such creatures as sea urchins, crabs, sea slugs, and purple abalone. The Marine Reserve is also full of hiking trails, but also various hazards, great and small, including high cliffs, sneaker waves, mountain lions, Lyme disease, poison oak, and the aforementioned white sharks.

Indeed, you're walking into the sharks' ocean estate, an area known as The Red Triangle. Imagine one vertice at Bodega Head, another southwest at the Farallon islands, and a third vertice at Monterey Bay. Pacific white sharks tend to gather along the north/central coast every fall and then depart in December on their way to a spot halfway between California and Hawaii. Researchers call this region "The White Shark Café." By one estimate, there are more than 220 adult great whites in the triangle, plus their pups. The adults often come close to shore. You can sometimes spot them around piers and inlets, often in the company of dolphins.

Address 2099 Westshore Road, Bodega Bay, CA 94923, +1 (707) 875-2211, www.marinescience.ucdavis.edu | Getting there By car, from US-101, take exit 488B to CA-12, drive 17 miles, and turn right onto CA-1. Then turn left onto Eastshore Road in Bodega Bay, and turn right onto Bay Flat Road, which becomes Westshore Road. Take a right onto the laboratory's entrance road past the campsite. | Hours See website for tour schedule | Tip Rent a kayak or paddle board from Bodega Bay Surf Shack and explore the estuaries or the bay (1400 N Highway 1, Bodega Bay, www.bodegabaykayak.com).

34___Burke's Canoe Trips

Paddling through heaven

The 110-mile Russian River flows out of the Laughlin Mountain Range east of Willits in Mendocino County, and southward through the Ukiah Valley. It eventually veers west, above Santa Rosa to Forestville, Guerneville, and the ocean. It's named for the Russian settlers who arrived in the early 1800s, although the Pomo Indians settled in the area 5,000 years before. One of the most bewitching stories tied to the river involves a historic landmark called Frog Woman Rock, which is filled with Pomo mythology. From certain angles, you can imagine an Indian face but with frog-like features.

This story has several versions, all beginning with Sotuka, the daughter of a Sanei Indian chief in a village near present-day Cloverdale. She falls in love with Concho, another chief's son who promises to marry her but then marries someone else. On their wedding night, the couple sleeps at the base of Frog Woman rock. Sotuka tracks them, hugs the largest rock she can, and hurls herself off a high ledge onto the sleeping newlyweds.

Frog Woman rock is also known for dangerous white-water rapids. The river's personality changes at the very popular stretch between Forestville and Guerneville, where you can swim or canoe. There are several places to rent equipment, among them Burke's Canoe Trips. For decades, this spot has been a popular jumping-off point for a 10-mile paddle by canoe or kayak. It takes a minimum of around five hours, and that's if you don't stop along the way at one of the tempting beaches. The river itself is glorious in most places, winding, sparkling, California lush, and, despite the drought, still maneuverable. Look for wildlife, especially herons.

The water can be knee-deep in some places or over your head in others. The current is generally slow, and in the late afternoon, when the wind picks up, you'll have to paddle hard. You'll feel it in your muscles the next day!

Address 8600 River Road, Forestville, CA 95436, +1 (707) 887-1222, www.burkescanoetrips.com | Getting there By car, from US-101, take exit 494 onto River Road west, continue for eight miles, and turn right onto Mirabel Road. | Hours Daily May–Sep 8am–11pm | Tip Just a half a mile west is Steelhead Beach, a popular summer destination for sunbathing, swimming, and picnicking (9000 River Road, Forestville, parks.sonomacounty.ca.gov/visit/find-a-park/steelhead-beach-regional-park).

35 __ Café Aquatica
Between the lagoon and the deep blue sea

The Russian River flows onto the Pacific Ocean through an estuary just below the village of Jenner. The estuary, or the lagoon in local parlance (they are not actually synonymous), includes eelgrass beds and mudflats and is a sanctuary for crab and various species of salmon, as well as seabird colonies. There's also a seasonal sandbar that divides ocean and estuary and attracts harbor seals for their daily "haul out." That's a daily ritual in which the seals beak away from foraging to molt and rest. They often sleep more than 10 hours. Interestingly, these haul-out areas may be segregated by age and sex even within the same species. You're likely to see seals in and around the estuary in the afternoon or early evening, particularly in April through June.

In Jenner, you'll find all the equipment you'll need to go kayaking, diving, and snorkeling, along with a wonderfully unexpected and very small restaurant with a calming view overlooking the lagoon. It's called Café Aquatica, and it features locally grown, organic ingredients. The menu has been recast in recent years to include a crab roll, a salmon bagel, matcha lattes, golden milk, a housemade granola bowl, and a pesto portobello mushroom sandwich served on focaccia bread. The café has picnic tables, and the wood is well-weathered. Sit out on the deck or the inside/outside area, or on the Adirondack chairs along the water banks.

Café Aquatica has become a community center and arts venue. Musicians from all over Sonoma County perform here every weekend, weather permitting. On some weekends and holiday afternoons, there's a classic jazz pianist and drummer. Events during the year include an afternoon with herbal infused 'mocktails'; open mics; radio concerts; a Makers Market with local crafts, including herbal remedies; and tarot readings by Sara Kalia Poliskin of Made In Moon Medicine – she's wildly popular.

Address 10439 Highway 1, Jenner, CA 95450, +1 (707) 865-2251, www.cafeaquaticajenner.com, cafeaquajenner@gmail.com | Getting there By car, rom US-101, take exit 479 and go west on Railroad Avenue. Turn right onto Stony Point Road, left onto Roblar Road, and right onto Valley Ford Road / CA-1. Continue 23 miles to the destination. | Hours Daily May–Oct 8am–5pm, Nov–Apr 8am–4pm | Tip Tasting By The Sea Wine Bar is right next door and offers tastings of wines produced by four local wineries (www.facebook.com/tastingbythesea).

36 California Indian Museum
Finding Ishi, "The Last Wild Indian in America"

The California Indian Museum and Cultural Center stands in an industrial park in Santa Rosa, an unlikely setting for such a tribute to the Indigenous cultures of California. But there it is, and well worth exploring. What makes this museum special is that it's an active community organization cast from a purely Native American perspective, as opposed to the Phoebe A. Hearst Museum of Anthropology at UC Berkeley, which is splendid, but not without all its ghosts. Moreover, the center is devoted to cultural growth, not oriented solely to the past but to the future. The goal is to affirm identity and pride among tribes from all over Northern California, to impart expertise, and to tell the stories. Younger Native Americans gather here to learn the art of museum curation, design, and management.

The museum includes a noteworthy collection of baskets, a canoe made of reeds, walnut dice, obsidian arrowheads, and also pans and irons that Native Americans were able to gather in their war with gold miners.

The dark history of the "war of extermination" on tribes in California is best understood through the life of Ishi, sometimes callously labeled "The Last Wild Indian in America." His story is the subject of the main exhibit in the museum and a reason to visit in and of itself. Ishi was a member of the Yahi Tribe, which was wiped out in the early 20th century. In 1911, Ishi, then in his 50s, was found hiding in a barn outside Oroville, north of Sacramento. He was arrested and eventually turned over to anthropologists at UC Berkeley, who turned him into a sideshow that benefited both the university and professors. He was given a room in the museum and paid $25 a month to be both a janitor and a human exhibition. He could be seen walking in Golden Gate Park or hunting on Mt. Parnassus. He died in 1916, and his last words were reportedly, "You stay, I go."

Address 5250 Aero Drive, Santa Rosa, CA 95403, +1 (707) 579-3004, www.cimcc.org, cimcc.interns@gmail.com | Getting there By car, from US-101, take exit 495 onto Airport Boulevard E and then turn right onto Aero Drive. | Hours Mon–Fri noon–4pm, by appointment only | Tip Another museum to see more exhibits about Native American cultures is Grace Hudson Museum, a one-hour drive north from Santa Rosa (431 S Main Street, Ukiah, www.gracehudsonmuseum.org).

37 __ California Mission Museum

Mission history in miniature

In 1769, just seven years before the US announced its independence, King Charles III of Spain authorized an expedition led by Franciscan padres to colonize the western edge of the Spanish empire. The strategy was to build a 650-mile-long string of 21 missions and four forts, known as *presidios*, to spread Catholicism to Indigenous peoples along the California coast, and at the same time establish an armed, cultural, and economic presence. The entire campaign lasted until 1823.

The southernmost mission was built in what is now San Diego, and the northernmost and last mission to be built was in the town of Sonoma. The missions were built roughly a day's walk apart. The architecture was distinguished by thick adobe bricks, terra-cotta tile roofs, and enclosed patios with fountains and gardens. One legacy of this period was the seeding of the cities of San Diego, Santa Barbara, San Jose, and San Francisco.

You can discover the history of these missions in miniature in the California Mission Model Museum, located on the grounds of the Cline Family Cellars just south of the Sonoma Valley airport. The owners of the vineyard acquired all of the models in 1998 and opened the museum in 2005. The exhibit is housed in a space built for the collection and two stained-glass panels that came from Mission Dolores in San Francisco prior to the 1906 earthquake and discovered during the mission's restoration. This main building houses the scale models of 16 missions, while a second building contains the other five.

The models, made of wood, clay, and paperboard, were created by German craftsmen under the direction of the Italian artist Leon Bayard de Volo for the Golden Gate International Exposition held at Treasure Island in 1939. The museum includes paintings of each mission, capturing them then and now.

Address 24737 Arnold Drive, Sonoma, CA 95476, +1 (707) 939-8051, californiamissionsmuseum.com | Getting there By car, from US-101, take exit 460 onto Sears Point Road / CA-37 E and then turn left onto Arnold Drive / CA-121. | Hours Daily 10am–6pm | Tip While you are there, sip and stroll around the beautiful grounds of family-owned Cline Cellars (www.clinecellars.com).

38 California School of Herbal Studies

Founded in the tradition of Western herbalism

The culinary empire north of San Francisco includes institutes, schools, labs, programs, spectacular gardens, the finest markets, the most exotic restaurants, and 'tasteries', along with 'food retreats', where you can contemplate the meaning of food, its derivations, how to honor various food traditions, and, of course, the work and joy at the foundation of it all.

One of these places is The California School of Herbal Studies (CSHS). It was started in 1978 by Rosemary Gladstar, a renowned author, lecturer, and activist, who also founded United Plant Savers, a nonprofit organization in Ohio dedicated to the preservation of North American medicinal plants. She is the creator of the home study video course 'The Science and Art of Herbalism'.

CSHS is set on 80 forested acres two miles from Forestville. The school campus includes a comfortable kitchen, a classroom, lab, and apothecary, and a half-acre garden featuring 400 herb species, plus terrific hiking trails. The school's mission is to "help create sustainable communities by providing an earth-centered, community-based education." The pedagogy is rooted in North American and European herbs, as well as Ayurvedic and Chinese plants. Classes include "Herbal Remedies for Parasites, Molds, and Yeasts," "The Magic and Science of Medicinal Mushrooms," and "Traditional Herbal Allies for Women, for All Phases of Our Lives."

Most classes are held at the school, and others are online. There are single-day workshops and two-day classes. More expansive courses go for two consecutive days once a month for several months, such as the introductory course on herbal support for the human body. You can also enroll in a two-year certification program that is highly regarded in the herbalism community.

Address 9309 Pocket Canyon Highway, Forestville, CA 95436, +1 (707) 887-7457, www.cshs.com | Getting there By car, from US-101, take exit 494 onto River Road west, and continue eight miles. Turn left onto Mirabel Road and right onto Pocket Canyon Highway/CA-116. | Hours See website for class schedule | Tip Step back in time at Ideal Hardware, with its old wooden floor, full shelves, and friendly service (6631 Front Street, Forestville).

39__Charles M. Schulz Museum

The gang's all here

Charles Schulz, the beloved cartoonist, was a satirist, an optimist, a keen observer of the times, and an obsessive entrepreneur. He was also, arguably, a moralist, although not in a sanctimonious way. He espoused a philosophy of simple happiness and genuine hope, and occasionally mild ridicule. His strips often combine a casual nuance with a comic drama. For example, in one cartoon, Snoopy is lying asleep on top of his doghouse, and Charlie Brown says, "My dog is home," This simple comment conveys the idea that all's right with the world.

Charles Schulz (1922–2000) was born in Minnesota and served in World War II. He moved to Sebastopol in 1958 and 10 years later to Santa Rosa. The two-story Charles M. Schulz Museum & Research Center opened in 2002. It is a state-of-the-art airy space befitting a famous artist and his fortune, and yet it's quite intimate. The collection includes thousands of original works, including "warm-up" sketches that a mindful assistant retrieved from the trash, as well as letters, photographs, and unique Peanuts products.

You might begin on the second floor with a biographical gallery and a recreation of Schulz' studio, including his personal library. You'll see books by James Thurber, Bill Mauldin, and a biography of Charlie Chaplin. Those you'd expect, but Schulz also read Joyce Carol Oates, Dashiell Hammett, and James Ellroy, as stark and dark a mystery writer as you'll find. Schulz also had a taste for classic films and watched *Citizen Kane* 40 times. The library and its archives are open to researchers wishing to look deeply into Schulz, life and work.

The museum's first floor includes galleries with rotating exhibitions. This is where you'll find strips done by contemporaries whom Schulz admired, including Bill Watterson, creator of *Calvin and Hobbes*. Be sure to look for Snoopy's doghouse "wrapped" by the artist Christo.

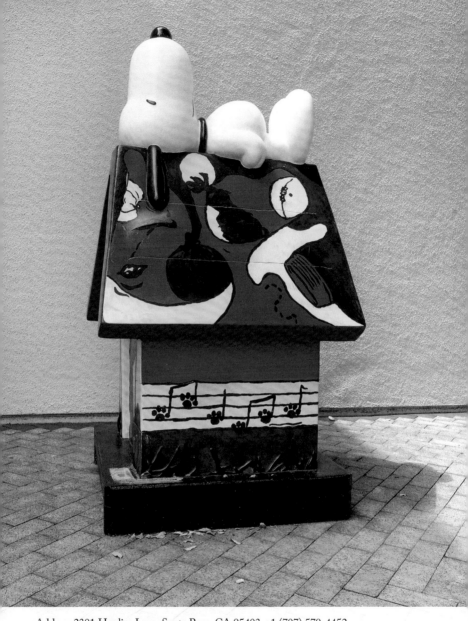

Address 2301 Hardies Lane, Santa Rosa, CA 95403, +1 (707) 579-4452, www.schulzmuseum.org, inquiries@schulzmuseum.org | **Getting there** By car, from US-101, take exit 49, follow Guerneville Road to W Steele Lane, and then turn right onto Hardies Lane. | **Hours** Mon–Fri 11am–5pm, Sat & Sun 10am–5pm | **Tip** Next to the museum is Snoopy's Home Ice, an enormous, year-round hockey rink built by Schulz with an exterior reminiscent of a Tyrolean chalet (1667 W Steele Lane, Santa Rosa, www.snoopyshomeice.com).

40 Children's Bell Tower
The Nicholas Effect

In September 1994, Margaret and Reginald Green took their two small children Eleanor and Nicholas on vacation to Calabria in Southern Italy. They were not aware that the Salerno-Reggio Calabria road at night was the province of thieves, including members of the *Ndrangheta* crime gang. Driving a rental car at 10:30pm, the Greens stopped briefly along the road at an Autogrill and then continued on. That was when Reginald noticed they were being followed.

Thieves saw the Greens at the Autogrill and marked them as wealthy foreigners. The bandits pulled alongside Green, and a masked man called out. Reginald instinctively accelerated. Twice, the bandits fired shots into the back of Green's car. Green made a run for it and eventually reached a roadblock. That was when he looked into the back seat to see that seven-year-old Nicholas had been shot in the head. The boy was declared brain dead two days later. The shooters were caught and eventually sent to prison.

Upon Nicholas' death, the Greens donated his organs in Italy to seven people awaiting transplants, four of them teenagers. The Greens received sincere gratitude from the Italian people, and they were received by Italy's then president. As a result of what is now called "The Nicholas Effect," organ donations in Italy have since tripled.

Among the monuments to Nicholas is the Children's Bell Tower in Bodega Bay. It's just off Route 1, behind a community garden, down a path that winds to the beach. In among the cypress and eucalyptus trees, you come to an 18-foot tall, three-tier, steel sculpture with 140 bells, donated mostly by Italian churches and schools. The center bell, blessed by Pope John Paul II, is inscribed with the names of the seven organ recipients. It's austere and compelling. It's also the kind of place you could bring your own grief, whatever it might be, and give it to the bells.

Address 2255 N Highway 1, Bodega Bay, CA 94923, www.nicholasgreen.org | Getting there By car, from US-101, take exit 488B to CA-12, and after 17 miles, turn right onto CA-1 to Bodega Bay. | Hours Unrestricted | Tip Take a moment and contemplate among sand dunes and the ocean at Bodega Dunes Beach (2485 N Highway 1, Bodega Bay, www.parks.ca.gov).

41 Christo's Running Fences

An artistic comment on division

Christo and his wife Jean-Claude, who were born on the same day in 1935, are best known for transforming landmarks into temporary palettes. Some of their installations stayed up just a week or two. Sometimes, the idea was to suggest a complementary relationship between humanity and nature or the contrast between water and land.

One of their most dramatic installations was a 5.5-meter-high, 39-kilometer-long fence, a four year project unveiled in 1976. For 14 days, it ran through the hills and valleys of Sonoma and Marin counties, from a spot near Highway 101 to the coast, where it disappeared into the ocean close to Bodega Bay. The fence itself was made of white nylon panels hung from steel cables attached to steel poles. The poles were dug three feet into the ground and supported by guy wires. The fence crossed 14 roads, 59 ranches and the desks of countless administrators, judges, journalists, artists, and advocates. The project was highly contentious.

There are two places you can visit to experience their art in the region. One is the Christo & Jeanne-Claude Running Fence Park at the Watson School State Park near Bodega (not to be confused with Bodega Bay). You'll find a closed, one-room schoolhouse built in 1856, and the park is nearby. There are some picnic tables and a view for a nice stop on a trip up the coast.

The second place to go is the Museum of Sonoma County in Santa Rosa, which is always worth a visit. But, above all, catch the Christo exhibit there, with more than 100 drawings, sculptures, collages, and photographs. It's worth noting that the real story of Christo and Jean Claude's creations is how they brought local communities into each project. As a dairy farmer told *Sonoma Magazine* in 1972, Christo "didn't get *Running Fences* built because he sold everybody on the idea. They got behind him because they liked and trusted him."

Address Watson School State Park: 14550 Bodega Highway, Bodega, CA 94922, +1 (707) 875-3540, parks.sonomacounty.ca.gov, parks@sonoma-county.org; Museum of Sonoma County: 425 7th Street, Santa Rosa, CA 95401, +1 (707) 579-1500, www.museumsc.org | Getting there Park: by car, from US-101, take exit 488 onto CA-12 toward Sebastopol and drive eight miles to the destination on the left side; Museum: by car, from US-101, take exit 490 onto College Avenue toward downtown Santa Rosa, turn right onto Mendocino Avenue, right onto Healdsburg Avenue, and right onto 7th Street. | Hours Park: daily dawn−dusk; Museum: Wed−Sun 11am−5pm | Tip Valley Ford Market is a "farmers' and rancher's grocery store," where you can find anything from food and local wines to plumbing fixtures and fishing tackle (14400 Coast Highway, Valley Ford).

42___The Church of One Tree

Believe it or not

Santa Rosa, a town of fewer than 200,000, has become a hub of the Sonoma hinterlands north of Marin County in the last 20 years. Downtown retains its Midwestern demeanor. Noteworthy historical sites include horticulturist Luther Burbank's home, gardens, and cemetery.

Also here is the Church of One Tree, a one-time Baptist church first located on Ross and B street before it was relocated to its current home on Sonoma Avenue. The church's front façade actually faces away from the street and towards Juilliard Park, with a small grove of redwood trees separating the church from the park. It's a five-minute walk to the Burbank gardens and the SOFA neighborhood. SOFA Santa Rosa Art District is home to nearly 40 working artists' studios and a number of galleries.

The church was built in 1873 from a single redwood tree taken from the Armstrong grove in Guerneville. The tree was 275 feet long and, judging by the age of other trees in the grove, more than 1,000 years old. Among the builders was Isaac Ripley, whose son Robert Ripley founded *Ripley's Believe It or Not!* Ripley Sr.'s wife was a parishioner here.

In 1970, the church was recast as the Robert L. Ripley Memorial Museum. Memorabilia from Robert Ripley (1890–1949) included his original cartoon drawings, as well as passports, a suitcase, a wax statue of Ripley, a pair of bedroom slippers, and odd anecdotes, including a "Believe It or Not" entry about a farmer who was run over by his tractor. The accident enabled the cure for the farmer's arthritis. The church was also featured in one of Ripley's earliest installments of *Believe It or Not!*

The church is now owned by the city and was restored in 2009. The museum is gone, but the church is often used for weddings and other events. The joyous interior has cathedral ceilings and hardwod floors. Light streams through the original stained-glass windows.

Address 492 Sonoma Avenue, Santa Rosa, CA 95401, +1 (707) 543-3285, www.srcity.org/633/Church-of-One-Tree | Getting there By car, from US-101, take exit 489 onto 3rd Street towards downtown Santa Rosa, then turn right onto Santa Rosa Plaza, and left onto Sonoma Avenue. | Hours By appointment only | Tip Visit Historic Railroad Square nearby with shops, restaurants and shopping, dining, entertainment, and landmark railway buildings from the early 1900s (4th Street, Santa Rosa, www.railroadsquare.net).

43 Cornerstone Sonoma Gardens

A country souk for flowers and greenery

Just up the street from the Sonoma County Airport, Cornerstone Sonoma is a marketplace with specialty stores, restaurants, a café, winery tasting rooms – and some very special gardens. Roam among the group of 10 intriguing showplace gardens created by landscape architects from all over the world. Each one is a tableau, a garden "room" carefully tuned with trees, plants, exotic trellises, pergolas, unusual sculptures, and the occasional water feature.

The gardens could leap straight out from the pages of *Sunset Magazine*. Indeed, five of the gardens are owned and managed by *Sunset*, which has been California's pre-eminent home design and garden publication since 1898. The magazine bought the space at Cornerstone in 2015 and divided the quarter acre into five themed garden rooms. The gardens themselves are designed by Homestead Design Collective as part of the magazine's effort to experiment and develop new gardening techniques and use the information not only for home gardens but in community gardens as well. In 2016, the Collective launched a community garden in San Mateo with 99 raised beds, which they use as a rallying point to educate residents of a local housing community to the benefits of urban gardening.

The gardens at Cornerstone reflect different motifs, all generally oriented to habitat and food. There's a Cocktail Garden, a Farm Garden, the Gathering Space, a Backyard Orchard, and the Flower Room. Spend some time strolling through all of them. You'll find art installations here, as well as chairs and benches where you can sit and contemplate, or maybe even enjoy a snack from the marketplace.

Though on a much smaller scale, the Cornerstone gardens and the way they're laid out may remind you of the annual garden festival at Château-de-Chaumont in the Loire Valley.

Address 23570 Arnold Drive, Sonoma, CA 95476, +1 (707) 933-3010, www.cornerstonesonoma.com, info@cornerstonesonoma.com | Getting there See website for garden tours, venues, and events. | Hours By car, from US-101, take exit 472B onto CA-116 E toward Sonoma, turn right onto Arnold Drive and then left onto Wagner Road. | Tip Shop for a fire pit, a bird bath, and other home goods at Potter Green & Co. at Cornerstone (23586 Arnold Drive, Sonoma, www.pottergreen.com).

44__ Cotati's Hexagonal Center

A town distinguished by defiance

Cotati is a quirky little town of 7,500, named after a Pomo Indian chief. Or such is the lore. The town, just south of Rohnert Park, derives much of its character from the 1960s and 70s, when it was known for coffee houses filled with musicians and political activists, such as The Last Great Hiding Place, a popular hotbed that gave birth to the "Cotati Counterculture." This movement drew people from all over the area and even had its own style, known as the "Cotati look," based on clothes you got at the Freestone, a free thrift store that lasted until 1983.

The beat goes on at La Plaza Park, a long-time downtown venue for summer music festivals. For years the star of the show was Jim Boggio (1939–1996). *Keyboards Magazine* named him "one of the three finest accordion stylists" in the country. The park features a bronze statue of the jolly man in action, playing his Petosa accordion. Boggio was a cofounder and an organizer of the Cotati Accordion Festival, usually the last weekend in August, where you can hear anything accordion, from zydeco and polka to conjunto.

Cotati has one other feather. Its city center was designed in the shape of a hexagon. This was in the 1890s, when the hexagon seemed a clever alternative to the rectangular gridiron. The grid, particularly in residential areas, had become unpopular because of its monotony, the ubiquitousness of pavement, and safety issues from through traffic. Proponents claimed the hexagon used shorter roads and utility lines and provided more green space. It also provided health benefits. If the hexagon is pointed due north, in theory, no room in a house would have a northern exposure. That was significant at the time because direct sunlight was thought to cure tuberculosis. Cotati's hexagon is one of two such designs in America – the other is Detroit.

Address 8167 La Plaza, Cotati, CA 94931 | **Getting there** By car, from US-101, take exit 481 onto W Sierra Avenue toward Cotati, and then turn right onto La Plaza. | **Hours** Unrestricted | **Tip** Go thrift shopping at Jewels to Junk and create your own Cotati look (8025 Gravenstein Highway, Cotati).

45 Creekside Park
Urban ornaments in the forest

As you come out of the redwoods along Highway 116, between Guerneville and Duncans Mills, you'll reach Monte Rio. It's a blip of a burg known for an old movie theater fashioned from a Quonset hut, a popular public beach along the Russian River, a famous golf course, and an annual variety show that's been playing on and off since 1912. And of course, nearby in the Bohemian Grove, there's the Bohemian Club, that ever secretive grotto for the wealthy and powerful.

Altogether, Monte Rio is a retro town with the feel of a 1950s roadside attraction. It's an unassuming haven for trades people, political independents, and isolationists. In recent years, though, the town has dusted itself off, become spiffy and cool.

Monte Rio is known for its beach, where you can rent kayaks, canoes, and inner tubes, and then laze about on the river, which is knee-deep or so in the summer. It's less crowded than the beaches in Guerneville. Down the way, in a bend in the river, you'll find Creekside Park, an unusual mixture of "activity and quietude," as locals describe it. In 2014, the town recast a rundown, flood-ravaged elementary school into a multi-use public park, which features a communal orchard and a fenced-in farm, where the produce includes blueberries, apples, figs, plums, and walnuts. There's also a pollinator garden to attract bees and butterflies.

There are several spots that are popular with children, namely a "park-approved" art wall on the back of the main building, where you'll see local masters at work, and a skatepark, the only one in the Russian River area. Elements include a bowl, taco, and snake run, designed for both novices and advanced skaters.

The four-acre park, which is encircled by a third-of-a-mile walking path known as the Dutch Bill Creek Loop Trail, is anchored by the Lightwave Coffee and Kitchen, a community favorite.

Address 9725 Main Street, Monte Rio, CA 95462, +1 (707) 865-2487, www.mrrpd.org/
creekside-park | Getting there By car, from US-101, take exit 494 onto River Road and
continue 19 miles. Turn left onto Church Street, right onto Fir Road, and left onto Main
Street. | Hours Unrestricted | Tip Russian River Cycle Services will deliver hybrid or road
bikes to you in Monte Rio, as well as a helmet, pump, basket, and lock (6559 Front Street,
Forestville, www.russianrivercycles.com).

46_ The Donum Estate

At the intersection of fine wine and fine art

A *donum* is derived from a Turkish word referring to a parcel of land measuring about an acre in size. Another meaning suggests a "gift of the land." The latter has become the motto of one of the valley's most distinguished wineries, the 200-acre Donum Estate in the Carneros wine region just southeast of Sonoma. It was founded in 2001 by Mei and Allan Warburg, art collectors who live between Hong Kong and Beijing. The estate's yield is a limited production of pinot noir and chardonnay grapes from 150 acres planted across vineyards in Carneros, the Russian River, the Sonoma Coast, and Mendocino County. Production runs to 10,000 cases of wine each year.

One of the unique features of this winery is the art collection, which includes some 50 sculptures. About one third are commissioned to be shown in particular parts of the vineyard in Carneros. Artists from 18 nations are represented here in one of the world's largest private sculpture collections. Renowned works include Ai Weiwei's *Circle of Animals / Zodiac Heads* (2011), Robert Indiana's iconic sculpture *LOVE*, and Doug Aitken's *Sonic Mountain (Sonoma)*, a tonal installation powered by 365 wind chimes. Also note Yue Minjun's *Contemporary Terracotta Warriors* standing in the tall grass. Olafur Eliasson's *Vertical Panorama Pavilion* is an unusual space inspired by circular calendars. Its roof is a spectacular, conical canopy resting on 12 stainless-steel columns and made from 832 recycled translucent glass panels in 24 colors.

Mr. Warburg told *ARTnews* in February 2021 that the inspiration to acquire all these pieces came from wanting to create "a combination of wine, art, and landscape." He said, "It's just such a different experience than being in a museum." He also explained that he doesn't look at art as a business. "I'm a collector," he continued in *ARTnews*. "I've never sold anything." As you stroll through the vineyards and admire the entire collection, you will understand exactly what he means.

Address 24500 Ramal Road, Sonoma, CA 95476, +1(707) 732-2200,
www.thedonumestate.com, hospitality@thedonumestate.com | Getting there By car,
from CA-121/Fremont Drive take Ramal Road S. | Hours Daily 10am–4pm by
appointment | Tip Take your own photo of the iconic Bliss Hill, which was used as
Windows XP's default desktop wallpaper and is one of the world's most viewed images
(3054 Fremont Drive, Sonoma).

47 Duncans Mills

On the banks of the Slavyanka

Russian settlers named the Slavyanka Waterway, which means "beautiful stream." Later, it simply became the Russian River, once famous for overflowing its banks, though not so much anymore. By 1877, two Scottish brothers Alex and Samuel Duncan opened a successful sawmill, but after being flooded out more than a dozen times, the brothers floated their mill upstream, along with a post office to add a sense of permanence to their new home, Duncans Mills. Then along came the 1906 earthquake, which caused three of the town's grand hotels to collapse, and the populace left, never to return. In 1935, the train that had enabled the creation of the town stopped service. The town disappeared.

But it reemerged in the 1970s. In 1971, the train station from 1907 was renovated and would win a statewide award for best restoration of a historic place. Today, Duncans Mills, with a population of under 200, has its own climate. Located just five miles from the coast, it often enjoys blue skies, even when fog is wrapped around the hills.

Aside from the weather, the town also has quite a few more delights to offer. The annual rodeo is the town's pride. It typically happens every fourth weekend in July and includes barrel racing, bronco busting, and bull riding. There is also a rustic marketplace designed around a quaint collection of classic Western-style galleries, eateries, and a train museum. Look for the distinguished North Pacific narrow gauge passenger car built in St. Louis in 1903. Recently, it's been recast as the town library.

Visit Twice as Nice for antiques, and The Poet's Corner Book Shop to find new and used books. The General Store offers great deli foods, and Christopher Queen Galleries has a fine selection of California art. Stop by the Cape Fear Café for a bite, or the Blue Heron, dating back to the 1800s and "the oldest tavern on the Russian River."

Address Duncans Mills, CA 95430, www.duncansmillsvillage.com | **Getting there** By car, from US-101, take exit 494 onto River Road W, continue for 24 miles, and turn right onto B Street in Duncans Mills. | **Hours** Unrestricted | **Tip** Duncans Mills Tea Shop has 100 kinds of loose leaf teas, along with pots, kettles, and paraphernalia, both antique and modern (25185 Main Street, Duncans Mills, www.duncansmillsteashop.com).

48 El Molino Central

Delicious innovating using ancient techniques

In Boyes Hot Springs, at Central Avenue, a few minutes west of downtown Sonoma, you'll find a small, classical Mexican restaurant called El Molino Central. Look for the line out the door, but don't let it deter you. You'll place your order inside and walk through the buzzing kitchen or around the building to a cantina-style covered patio. The food is amazing. Customer favorites include the halibut ceviche with house-made chips, the red mole tamales, Bohemia beer-battered cod tacos, and poblano-tomatillo nachos verdes. For vegetarians, the butternut squash enchiladas are divine. The tortillas are moist, thick, and slightly sweet. Entrees change with the seasons.

The masa for the tamales and corn tortillas is ground right here – one of the secrets to their success. Getting the texture right is tricky, and they know how to do it by using a mill to grind nixtamalized corn – or dried corn that's been simmered in an alkaline bath and then washed and hulled, all by hand – into masa. It's the ancient way of making masa from Central America. So remember this trick the next time you're making your own masa.

El Molino's owner Karen Taylor Waikiki is the person responsible for the whole operation. Thirty years ago, she was influenced by Diana Kennedy's classic cookbook, *The Cuisines of Mexico*. Her passion for Mexican food took her traveling all over Mexico, and she opened El Molino Central in June 2010. She credits her restaurant's success to her crew, many of whom come from different states in Mexico. Sometimes she'll recreate dishes based on recipes her crew learned from their own mothers.

Her original company Primavera has been selling organic stone-ground tortillas and tamales at farmers' markets around the Bay Area. You can try samples of El Molino's dishes plus crispy chips and tangy salsa to take home every Saturday at the Ferry Plaza Farmers Market in San Francisco.

Address 11 Central Avenue, Sonoma, CA 95476, +1 (707) 939-1010, www.elmolinocentral.com | Getting there By car, from W Napa Street in Sonoma, take CA-12 north two miles, and turn right onto Central Avenue. | Hours Mon–Thu 11am–8pm, Fri–Sun 9am–8pm | Tip Take a walk on some easy trails alongside Sonoma Creek at dog-friendly Maxwell Farms Regional Park (100 Verano Avenue, Sonoma, parks.sonomacounty.ca.gov).

49 Erickson Fine Art Gallery

Representing the best of local artists

In the last 30 years, pent-up wealth in the Bay Area has pushed ever further north. What were once small, getaway towns at the turn of the 20th century have acquired an air of trendy and cosmopolitan permanence. Take Healdsburg, for example, 15 minutes north of Santa Rosa. The town has established an arts identity and is in the process of implementing an ambitious Community Arts Culture Master Plan.

Among the best-known fine art galleries in this part of northern California is Erickson Fine Art Gallery, located in a three-story, Palladio-style building on Healdsburg Avenue, just down the street from the town plaza. The gallery opened in San Francisco in 1983 and moved to Healdsburg in the late 1990s. It's owned by Sandy Erickson and her daughter Danielle Elins and focuses on internationally known Northern California artists in mid to late careers. The offerings include sculpture, mixed media, and contemporary paintings, from landscapes and figurative to abstract.

As you come to the gallery, note the flawlessly executed mobiles and kinetic works by the late Jerome Kirk. Also among the gallery's more popular artists is Antoinette von Grone, originally from Germany and best known for her animal portraiture distinguished by hyper realism mixed with whimsy. Her most compelling work includes classical 18th-century feasts in which the figures have animal bodies but very human expressions and gestures. Pride and class consciousness are common denominators, mixed with a touch of humor and intrigue.

Joe Draegert is best known for his magical realism still life, as well as his American and Italian landscapes. He won the Rome Prize in 1978. Fellow artist Wayne Thiebaut said about Draegert in 2010, that he had been pursuing a "life of crime," "building beautiful painted worlds of lies that reveal special truths about this real old world of ours."

Address 324 Healdsburg Avenue, Healdsburg, CA 95448, +1 (707) 431-7073,
www.ericksonfineartgallery.com, info@ericksonfineartgallery.com | Getting there
By car, from US-101, take exit 503 toward Central Healdsburg and continue onto
Healdsburg Avenue. | Hours Thu–Tue 11am-6pm | Tip For local history and artifacts,
visit Healdsburg Museum and Historical Society (221 Matheson Street, Healdsburg,
www.healdsburgmuseum.org).

50__ *The Expanding Universe*
A pacifist's missile-like peace obelisk

A 14-mile drive north from the town of Jenner on Highway 1, you'll reach Timber Cove. There's an upscale resort on the windy bluffs, with a quintessentially Northern California view of the Pacific. The property behind is one of the smallest California state parks, just a 60-foot circle with a sculpture designed by Italian artist Beniamino Bufano (1890–1970). He is best known for his animal sculptures, especially bears. His work is found all over Northern California.

His eight-story, 20-ton sculpture at Timber Cove is visible for miles and is alternately known as *The Madonna of Peace* or *The Expanding Universe*. At first glance, it suggests an ultra-modern totem pole, totally smooth, with images of the Madonna and child and an open hand at the very top. Considering Bufano's interest in world peace, along with the sculpture's slight lean – and the year it was created, 1962, just weeks before the Cuban missile crisis – you might also imagine a still life of an intercontinental ballistic missile at launch.

The work is made largely of redwood, lead, and concrete, as well as mosaic tiling, which was added by Alfonso Pardiñas (1924–1975), known as "the master of mosaics." He was the co-creator of this sculpture, although rarely credited. He was also a wildly popular bohemian in San Francisco. He is known for creating the golden domes and mosaics on the Russian Orthodox Church in San Francisco.

Bufano was a bit of a mystery. In *Bufano: An Intimate Biography* (1972), Bufano was quoted to say "I just told each person not only what I thought he wanted to hear, but I related it in the way I thought appropriate for him."

During World War I, Bufano, a well-known pacifist and colorful character, cut off part of his right index finger by accident. He sent it to President Wilson as an anti-war protest and allowed a myth to spread that he had severed it deliberately.

Address 21780 Highway 1, Jenner, CA 95450 | Getting there By car, from US-101, take exit 479 and go west on Railroad Avenue, turn right onto Stony Point Road, turn left onto Roblar Road, and turn right onto Valley Ford Road / CA-1. Continue 37 miles to the destination. | Hours Unrestricted | Tip You can spend the night at Timber Cove, which has 46 rooms, each with beautiful views of the ocean or the forest, or you can just stop by for a meal at their Coast Kitchen Restaurant (21780 Highway 1, Jenner, www.timbercoveresort.com).

51 The Fairy Doors
An urban myth for these times

Fifteen miles north of Santa Rosa, up Highway 101, you reach Healdsburg, a place that was once home to Pomo Indians. Nowadays, the small town settled along the Russian River is filled with historic houses and districts, and invariably lands on lists like "The Ten Most Charming Small Towns in America." On the square you'll find tasting rooms, clothing shops, art galleries, and high-end restaurants. The town is also firmly progressive, with state-of-the-art recycling, a noise abatement ordinance, and deep reverence for its riparian zone along the river.

The community also has some very special and very tiny attractions. In 2017, Healdsburg drew attention for a phenomenon involving "fairy doors," which began appearing all over downtown. There are nearly 20 fairy doors that are roughly six inches high and three inches wide. They usually appear at ground level, and they look simply like special tiny entrances for very small fairy folk.

The architectural style of the doors often matches the "host" venue, and as the phenomenon has spread, the doors have become increasingly elaborate. The Stafford Gallery's fairy door, for example, reflects the overall Greek Revival theme of the building. Many doors in the countryside appear in trees. Some doors are decorated to reflect the season. Passersby leave acorns and coins.

A door "just magically appeared one day at our doorstep," Holly Hoods told the *Press Democrat* in 2018. She's the executive director of the Healdsburg Museum and Historical Society. "It looks like they were trying to replicate the museum door. It is as dignified as our restored Carnegie Library Building." Other lucky towns that host fairy doors include Alameda and Berkeley in Northern California; Ann Arbor, Michigan; Putnam, Connecticut; Milwaukee, Wisconsin; Detroit, Michigan; Hempstead, New York; Dublin, Ohio; and Donegal in Ireland, among others.

Address Various locations around Healdsburg, CA, www.healdsburg.com/media/1774/fairymap.pdf | Getting there By car, from US-101, take exit 503 toward Central Healdsburg and continue onto Healdsburg Avenue. | Hours Unrestricted | Tip Visit Gallery Lulo for beautiful jewelry, fine art, and other handmade treasures (303 Center Street, Healdsburg, www.gallerylulo.com).

52 Flamingo Hotel

She had long legs and red hair

The original Las Vegas Flamingo Hotel opened in December 1946. It was owned by the crime impresario Bugsy Siegel, who was shot to death several months later while sitting in his girlfriend's living room in Beverly Hills. A long-time rumor was that Siegel named the hotel after her because she had red hair and long legs. Another story is that Siegel once noticed the flamingos at the Hialeah horse track in Miami and believed they brought him good luck.

Inspired by the original namesake hotel, the Flamingo Resort in Santa Rosa opened on 10 acres in 1957. Visitors in those days included Jayne Mansfield and Frankie Avalon, – B-list movie stars then, but these days their names convey "high retro." The property languished for years as simply an eccentric neighborhood hotel, but in 2021, it received a $20 million makeover. Now, it's worth seeing even just to explore. The tone combines a mid-century style and a millennial vibe.

The resort, with its iconic Flamingo neon sign, is distinguished by several art installations. San Francisco artist Serge Gay Jr. created a larger-than-life mural showing a lobby receptionist named Monroe. A sculpture at the hotel entrance is by HYBYCOZO, a collaborative studio of two artists Serge Beaulieu and Yelena Filipchuk, who focus on geometric sculptures inspired by mathematical shapes. Also note the rope art installation in the resort's event foyer by San Francisco artist Windy Chien. She's best known for her 2016 book, *The Year of Knots*, based on her journey to learn a new knot every day for a year.

The resort is filled with nostalgic ambiance created by the color schemes and a sense of social responsibility. For example, rooms feature mint green Trimline telephones and matching tea kettles, and they also offer refillable glass water pitchers, as well as refillable toiletry dispensers to restrict plastics.

Address 2777 4th Street, Santa Rosa, CA 95405, +1 (415) 545-8530,
www.flamingoresort.com | Getting there By car, rom US-101, take CA-12 east to Farmers
Lane. | Hours See website for amenities and dining reservations. | Tip Enjoy an evening of
a live performance at Santa Rosa's Sixth Street Playhouse (52 W Sixth Street, Santa Rosa,
www.6thstreetplayhouse.com).

53 Flatbed Farm

From farm to fork

Alice Waters is widely considered the founder of the Farm-to-Table movement, which began to take root in the 1960s. Her restaurant in Berkeley is the illustrious Chez Panisse. Both the farmer and restaurateur can greatly benefit by stabilizing crop supply and demand, enhancing the local food supply, and helping protect the environment.

There are more than 3,500 farms in Sonoma County. The average size is around 158 acres. And many describe themselves as farm-to-table – or fork. One such place is a flourishing, 10-acre farm in the Sonoma Valley called Flatbed Farm, between the Bouverie Preserve and the Sonoma Regional Parkland in Glen Ellen. Flatbed was started in 2012 by Sophie and Chris Dolan, two urban professionals, as a weekend home. Gradually, they became mesmerized by the mystique of farming and a community built around sustainably grown food.

The farm includes fields, a chicken coop, a greenhouse, and a series of outer buildings used for various purposes. The original barn was destroyed in the wildfires of 2017.

Depending on the season, the farm produces various kinds of salad greens, fruits and flowers, herbs and eggs. A weekly farm stand, which is one of the vital features of this kind of community-oriented farm, offers starter plants and a pantry collection of items made on the farm, as well as gifts, like dried flowers, bath salts, and more.

Flatbed Farm supplies local restaurants. In addition, the farm is expanding its profile in the community. You can take classes in growing herbal teas, including how blends are made; workshops in wellness and flower arranging; and kitchen decoration. In addition, there are plans to invite guest speakers to talk about all aspects of this trend that includes not only farm-to-table operations, but also community engagement. For the special events the farm features a live band, a food truck and local artisans.

Address 13450 Sonoma Highway, Glen Ellen, CA 95442, www.flatbedfarm.com, info@flatbedfarm.com | Getting there By car, take CA-12 about seven miles north of Sonoma to the destination. | Hours Sat 9am–3pm | Tip Stop at Juanita Juanita for a delicious tortilla soup (19114 Arnold Drive, Sonoma, www.juanitajuanita.com).

54 Florence Avenue

A small town's outdoor 'junk art' gallery

Among the originators of so-called Junk Art, Robert Rauschenberg (1925–2008) comes to mind. And most people will immediately think of his work *Monogram* (1955–1959). That was the stuffed Angora goat he found at a used furniture store on Seventh Avenue in Manhattan in 1955. He negotiated the price from $35 to $15, took the creature to his studio, and began a series of iterations that included slipping a car tire around the goat's mid-section. Eventually, Rauschenberg stood the goat on an abstract painting, thus mixing painting and sculpture. He described it as a "combine."

Sixty years later, Junk Art has blossomed into new combines, especially with recycled objects. Northern California, especially north of San Francisco, has growing pockets of artists devoted to the virtues of recycling. In Healdsburg, for example, people at a local community center have gotten into "trashion fashion," using plastic items from the trash to make dresses.

But nowhere is this junk art trend more vivid than on a neighborhood street in Sebastopol, a 10-minute drive west of Santa Rosa. In front of every house on a stretch of Florence Avenue stands a combine in the form of a painted sculpture. This is "high folk art," witty, Pixar-ish, animalesque, and character driven. Imagine crows getting drunk at a *Crow Bar*. Far from Rauschenberg, but the real significance here is that this street is a gallery, and a source of community, whether you like the art or not.

It's all the work of Brigitte Laurent and Patrick Amiot. She's a painter, and he's a sculptor. "The whole purpose of my work," Amiot says on his website, "is to glorify these objects, because they have their own spirit. When a hubcap has traveled on a truck for millions of miles, and has seen the prairies in the winter and the hot summer asphalt, when it's done traveling with that truck and finds itself in the scrap yard and I find it, I like to use that."

Address Florence Avenue, Sebastopol, CA 95472, www.patrickamiot.com | Getting there
By car, from US-101, take exit 481B onto CA-116 W and continue eight miles to Florence
Avenue in Sebastopol. | Hours Unrestricted | Tip While driving down River Road along
the Russian River near Forestville, you'll find another collection of more than 100 colorful
quirky sculptures created by Davingy (River Road, Forestville, www.davingy.com).

55 Fort Ross

Foreshadowing of modernity

Fort Ross was set up by Russian people on the ancestral Kashia Pomo land, built over several years beginning in 1806 as part of an agricultural settlement. The idea was to find a spot unclaimed by Europeans and then plant flax and hemp, and breed horses and cattle. It became an international community of Native Kashia and Coast Miwok people, Siberian Sakha, Russians, Aleuts, and Spaniards. They all lived in relative harmony, which was a key factor in Fort Ross' success. However, their handling of the environment was more inauspicious. By 1817, the people here, including the British, the Americans, and the Spanish, had all but destroyed the sea otter population.

The fortress includes multiple buildings both inside and outside the gate. Outside, you will find the village site where Native Alaskans lived, brought by the Russian American Company to serve as hunters and workmen. There are four buildings inside the perimeter: a chapel, two blockhouses, living quarters for the camp manager, and an administration building. You can imagine the scenes in this compound, with its small, dark rooms filled with hunters, traders, ship captains, ship builders, farmers, and Alaskans. And there were people you might not expect, like Russian naturalists and scientists, who were among the earliest to record California's cultural and natural history, not to mention the designers and craftsmen who built California's first two windmills to grind wheat into flour.

The Russians also brought glass windows and stoves from Europe and the first vaccines in California. People from the empire – Ukrainians, Belarussians, Georgians, and others – were all bound by a common purpose. Fort Ross now is a historic landmark. As for the Native people of Fort Ross, a fraction of the Kashia Band of Pomo Indians still live nearby on the 40-acre reservation called Stewart Point Rancheria.

Address 19005 Highway 1, Jenner, CA 95450, +1 (707) 847-3286, www.parks.ca.gov | Getting there By car, from US-101, take exit 479 and go west on Railroad Avenue, turn right onto Stony Point Road, left onto Roblar Road, and right onto Valley Ford Road/CA-1. Continue 35 miles to the destination. | Hours Daily 10am–4:30pm | Tip Fort Ross Vineyard, five miles away, is the vineyard closest to the Pacific Coast in California (15725 Meyers Grade Road, Jenner, www.fortrossvineyard.com).

56__Freestone
Town of 32 artisans

Freestone, population 32, is nestled in a scenic valley among rolling hills of Western Sonoma. It was a lumber and stone town, originating from a land dispute that was resolved by General Mariano Vallejo in the 1830s. Nearly 200 years later, the town is a historic district distinguished by 19th-century, Western-style architecture, and by a community of genuine artisans who are both friendly and occasionally insular, often refugees from other parts of the Bay Area. Above all, these are people devoted to their crafts and to the values of sustainability, "right livelihood," "meaningful work," and social awareness.

"Downtown" Freestone stretches for barely a half mile, and it was named Sonoma County's first historic district in 1974. As you stroll down the street, you will find shops that celebrate artisan food and culture, such as Wild Flour Bread. The bakery is renowned in the area for its specialties, including insanely tasty sourdough loaves, sweet and savory scones, and biscotti baked in a wood-fired brick oven. You can stroll in their large garden in the back, where they grow fresh fruit, herbs, and vegetables. Another mainstay in the town is Freestone Artisan Cheese, which offers hand-crafted cheeses, California nuts, olive oils grown and pressed locally, raw honey, small-batch jams, crackers, panforte, chocolates, and charcuterie. Many of the cheeses come from Sonoma County artisan cheese makers, most within a 20-mile radius of the store.

There's also a Joseph Phelps Vineyard tasting room in Freestone, along with the Osmosis Day Spa. The latter has been in the area since the mid 1980s. Its signature treatment includes a unique cedar enzyme bath and a rejuvenating heat treatment developed in Japan, plus a long list of facials and massages. The grounds are quietly spectacular too, with Japanese gardens for some self-care and reflection.

Address Bohemian Highway, Freestone, CA 95472 | Getting there By car, from US-101, take exit 488B to CA-12, drive 12 miles, and then turn right onto Bohemian Highway. | Hours Unrestricted | Tip Less than five miles south of Freestone, you'll find the charming small town of Valley Ford and the historic 1864 Valley Ford Hotel (14415 Shoreline Highway, www.vfordhotel.com).

57 Goat Rock Beach

For meditations on time and impermanence

Let's say you need a time away, but not far away – merely a long afternoon somewhere unexpected to clear your head and calibrate clarity. A beach with a clear horizon, the steady rhythm of breaking waves, and perhaps geological revelations such as platforms, terraces, and stacks is just the place you seek. And so you drive up the coast to Goat Rock Beach. Actually, there are two beaches to consider off the same access road, Blind and Goat Rock. Dogs are allowed at Blind Beach, but not at Goat Rock.

Goat Rock itself is one of the most majestic features on this part of the coast. The lore is that early 20th-century goats grazed on the rock's flat top. (Climbing it is not permitted.) The ocean here is home to seals, sea lions, pelicans, and gray whales during migration cycles. Forty thousand years ago, wooly mammoths also lived here. The beach is pristine, blown clean by gusty winds. Note the piles of bleached white driftwood, which have been scrupulously collected by beachcombers and made into windbreaks and beach quarters. The sand at the shoreline is dark gray, smooth, and loose. It's the color of café au lait, but it's not a place to swim because of rip tides and sneaker waves. There's a single lifeguard station, but it's rarely manned. Except in high summer, there are few visitors here.

Geologically, the land is rising at a rate of one to three inches a century. At the same time, a yearly average of one to three feet of coastline slides into the sea. The San Andreas fault runs through here, and the geological drama is caused by tectonic plates colliding and forcing the creation of "sea stacks." The stacks are composed of various rock formations, including limestone and quartz, which erode at different rates to create these unusual forms. The relentless rub of water, wind, and sand over millions of years can redraw continents – something to ponder here.

Address Goat Rock Beach, Goat Rock Road, Jenner, CA 95450, www.parks.ca.gov | **Getting there** By car, from US-101, take exit 479 and go west on Railroad Avenue. Turn right onto Stony Point Road, left onto Roblar Road, and right onto Valley Ford Road/CA-1. Continue 22 miles and turn left onto Goat Rock Road. | **Hours** Daily dawn–dusk | **Tip** River's End Restaurant offers mesmerizing views of the coast, especially at sunset (11048 Highway 1, Jenner, www.ilovesunsets.com).

58 Gravensteins of Sebastopol

An apple with a highly strung nature

Some years ago, a *New York Times* reporter writing about the slow demise of the Gravenstein apple in Sonoma County pointed out that the name "Gravenstein" suggested a "Transylvanian undertaker." Certainly, it's an apple with strange roots. Originally, in the 17th century, it was grown around the Gräfenstein Castle in Denmark. It then found its way to Nova Scotia and then eventually to a patch of perfectly suited soil and weather in what is now Sonoma County. But how exactly did it get to California? Was it with the Russian settlers who came to Fort Ross in the early 1800s? It's a mystery.

What's sure is that in 1890, the great American horticulturist Luther Burbank urged his friend Nathaniel Griffith to grow Gravensteins around Sebastopol. Apparently, they didn't do well elsewhere in California. By the 1930s, Gravensteins from Sonoma were all the rage, and in 1940, there were nearly 10,000 acres of Gravensteins. That was the high. By 1950, there were only about 7,500 acres, and half that by 1980. In 2015, just 704 acres of Gravenstein trees remained.

One reason they have all but disappeared? The worldwide popularity of Gravensteins has driven down prices. So Sonoma farmers have inevitably turned to growing more profitable grapes.

Growers will tell you they're "ephemeral" and survive thanks to the menus of expensive restaurants, where they're used in apple sauce, juice, and apple pie.

Sebastopol and some surrounding towns have places where you can pick your own Gravensteins, such as Ragle Ranch Farm, which also hosts an annual festival. Another is Dutton Ranch, where Whole Foods and Trader Joe's get their apples. There is also Apple-A-Day Ratzlaff Ranch, Gabriel Farm, and Mom's Apple Pie, a local favorite bakery, where you can indulge in the delicious apple pie.

Address Mom's Apple Pie, 4550 Gravenstein Highway N, Sebastopol, CA 95472,
+1 (707) 823-8330, www.momsapplepieusa.com | Getting there By car, from US-101, take
exit 488B to CA-12 and turn right onto CA-116/Gravenstein Highway N in Sebastopol. |
Hours Daily 10am–6pm | Tip Shop at The Barlow in Sebastopol, a mixed use, outdoor
market in a former apple cannery with lots of shops and restaurants (6770 McKinley Street,
Sebastopol, www.thebarlow.net).

59__ The Green Music Center
Starring the Santa Rosa Symphony

To the thrill of all those who love classical music, the greater Bay Area is rich with symphony orchestras. Between Monterey and Santa Rosa, there are nearly a dozen of them, starting with the San Francisco Symphony, the fourth largest such musical organization in the country. The others are regional, and each of these local symphonies endures a delicate balance of public taste and expectation, union rules, conflicting creative visions, the longevity and loyalty of large donors, and the pull of other attractions. Perhaps most importantly, these venerable groups, particularly in the North Bay, realize that their success is closely tied to enticing tourists to venture out from San Francisco to enjoy a concert on a Saturday night or a Sunday afternoon.

There are two symphonies in Napa and Sonoma counties. Symphony Napa Valley plays at the Napa Valley Performing Arts Center in Yountville. The center is at the Lincoln Theater, which opened in 1957 on the grounds of the local veteran's home.

And then there's the Santa Rosa Symphony, which opened in 1928, when 35 musicians stepped out from behind the wings in an Elks Club. Since then, the symphony, based in Rohnert Park, has had a great run of musical directors and has established itself as a model of success as a regional orchestra. They reach 90,000 people a year with a variety of concert programs.

To be sure, an educated audience is critical to the success of any classical music enterprise, along with a tradition of highly talented music directors. But equally important is the venue itself. In 2012, the Santa Rosa Symphony made a clever move by becoming the resident orchestra of Sonoma State University's Green Music Center, with its 1,400-seat Weill Hall and 240-seat Schroeder Hall. Weill Hall is an architectural wonder and includes a rear wall that opens to a large lawn area for summer concerts. The Green Center presents artists all year long.

Address Sonoma State University, 1801 E Cotati Avenue, Rohnert Park, CA 94928, +1 (707) 664-4246, gmc.sonoma.edu, tickets@sonoma.edu | **Getting there** By car, from US-101, take exit 483 onto Rohnert Park Expressway and turn right onto East Redwood Drive. | **Hours** See website for performance schedule. | **Tip** Another venue to see music, dance, theater or comedy performances is the Luther Burbank Center for the Arts (50 Mark West Springs Road, Santa Rosa, www.lutherburbankcenter.org).

60__ The Hand Fan Museum
A fan history of culture

This is the kind of place you'd expect to find hidden away on a cob-blestone alley in downtown San Francisco, New York, Paris, or Tokyo. It's the Hand Fan Museum and shop, about the size of a large walk-in closet, and particularly well-lit for the purpose of admiring the design and details of these delicate objects of beauty. The walls and cases are filled with fans from all over the world and from various centuries and styles. They're made from wood, silk, parchment, bone, and paper. A mannequin here wears a dress made entirely from fans.

The Healdsburg museum is owned by a long-time collector named Pamela Sher. Fifty years ago, she followed an obsession with art history and began to focus on the artistry and culture of hand fans. She sifted through countless junk and antique stores, networked within hand fan associations, and attended auctions, including some at Drouot in Paris, "the world's oldest auction house," which holds special auctions devoted to fans.

Sher and her late husband Merritt had pugs, and so they began their collection with a 19th-century Viennese advertising fan fea-turing a pug. She once told *Marin Magazine* that her favorite fans in her collection include a *trompe l'oeil* design in which mice appear to be eating the fan itself, a 19th-century German fan made of ivory with carved lilies of the valley, and a 19th-century French satin leaf fan with painted roses.

This is the first museum in the US dedicated exclusively to hand fans, and it includes both a permanent collection and rotating exhibits. Fan history is rich. In 4,000 years, fans have been regarded as sacred objects. They have been used to cool the skin, serve as a coquette's tool, and advertise. In Japan, the fan has been used as a theatrical prop, a weapon, and a message board on the battlefield. Sher has designed her museum to be an active resource for lecturers and writers who wish to use fan history in the study of art history.

Address 309 Healdsburg Avenue, Healdsburg, CA 95448, +1 (707) 431-2500, www.thehandfanmuseum.org, handfanmuseum@icloud.com | Getting there By car, from US-101, take exit 503 toward Central Healdsburg and continue onto Healdsburg Avenue. | Hours Wed–Mon noon–5pm | Tip To relax and rejuvenate your body, make an appointment at A Simple Touch Spa (239 Center Street, Healdsburg, www.asimpletouchspa.com).

61 Hunter S. Thompson House

Fear and loathing in Sonoma

Hunter S. Thompson was the great "gonzo journalist." The meaning of gonzo comes from the Italian, meaning "simpleton." It's an unconventional style of journalism, where the writer is both protagonist and antagonist. Thompson's most famous work was *Fear and Loathing in Las Vegas: A Savage Journey to the Heart of the American Dream*. His perspective was always raw and from the counterculture, even if one of his favorite writers, F. Scott Fitzgerald, was the opposite of gonzo.

In 1964, at age 27, he moved from Woody Creek, Colorado to Glen Ellen. He arrived with his pregnant wife Sandra and was immediately told the promised rental he'd arranged was no longer available. It was the beginning of a terrible year, but they would later enjoy several great years.

Eventually, Hunter and Sandra found a small ranch house at 9400 Bennett Valley Road, nowadays just a white fenced area overgrown with California oak trees. They named their new home Owl House, in tribute to Jack London's Wolf House. Their son Juan Fitzgerald Thompson was born at Santa Rosa Memorial Hospital.

Thompson's Glen Ellen period was a time of intense self-doubt. He wrote to a friend that he was nearly destitute, lived in a shack, and was bound by depression and a desire for revenge, although against whom and why wasn't clear. He was broke, and in order to pay the rent, he pawned his belongings. Eventually, he picked up some magazine writing assignments at the *National Review*. One of his finest pieces from this period explored Ernest Hemingway's suicide.

Among the places Thompson frequented in Glen Ellen was a bar called the Rustic, which was destroyed in a 1974 fire. He described it as a pastoral den with the mixed vibes of a sanctuary for orderlies at the local asylum, as well as a hangout for accomplished ne'er-do-wells.

Address 9400 Bennett Valley Road, Glen Ellen, CA 95442 | Getting there By car, from Sonoma, take Arnold Drive north, turn left onto Warm Springs Road, and then turn left onto Bennett Valley Road. | Hours Viewable from the outside only | Tip Visit Vito and Guido Vino, "Brothers of the Grape" and best friends for over 50 years, at Two Amigos Winery (2750 Johns Hill Road, Glen Ellen, www.twoamigoswines.com).

62 Isis Oasis Temple & Sanctuary

Reclaiming ancient wisdom

Neopaganism, as you find it in Northern California, seems less visible in recent years. The 1990s and early 2000s was a time when, on the Summer Solstice, you could go to a certain glade in Golden Gate Park in San Francisco and join a ritual guided by Starhawk, the great pagan feminist figure, who has done so much to articulate a vision of the world as "one living organism."

Another local neopagan figure from that era is Loreon Vigne (1932–2014), best known as the founder of the Isis Oasis Temple and Sanctuary in Geyserville. She bought 10 acres in 1978 and founded her church. It was formally recognized by the State of California in 1996. The land originally belonged to Pomo Native Americans, then the Baha'i School, and now followers of the Egyptian Goddess Isis, who in modern times represents Mother Earth. In Egyptian mythology, Isis was the wife of Osiris and known for her ability to resurrect the dead.

The sanctuary is dedicated to "the divine feminine" and remains one of the few neopagan refuges of its kind. It's a few minutes' drive up Highway 101 from Healdsburg. deTraci Regula, the high priestess of the sanctuary, describes the place as an "Egyptian-themed retreat center" that offers lectures, meditations, the annual Inner Sanctum Symposium, and daily rituals, notably a noon day prayer. On Tuesdays, the prayer is directed at those who have passed, including animals. Accommodations include a lodge, with a dozen rooms that have access to a pool, sauna, and spa. There are also cabins and "hobbit huts" made of adobe bricks, in the style of ancient Egypt. Don't miss the exotic animal sanctuary. Animals being cared for here include African crowned cranes, a bearded dragon, rare pheasants, white-and-blue peacocks, and boa constrictors, among others.

Address 20889 Geyserville Avenue, Geyserville, CA 95441, +1 (707) 857-4747, www.isisoasissanctuary.org | Getting there By car, from US-101, take exit 510 and turn right onto Geyserville Avenue. | Hours Mon–Sat 9am–5pm, Sun 10am–5pm | Tip Francis Ford Coppola Winery also serves as a museum of Coppola's movie memorabilia, including his Oscars and Marlon Brando's desk from *The Godfather* (300 Via Archimedes, Geyserville, www.francisfordcoppolawinery.com).

63 Korbel Gardens

A blend of bubbly and roses

Korbel, the top selling domestic sparkling wine in the US, was started by three Czech brothers named Francis, Anton, and Joseph Korbel. They were political activists, rascals, and savvy businessmen, who began their careers by making cigars and then cigar boxes. They arrived in San Francisco in 1862, where they followed an interest in wood to build their cigar boxes. They would expand into shipbuilding, farming, and eventually winemaking. They purchased land in many locations, but the property at the Russian River provided redwood used for their cigar box business. They built a connecting railway to ship the boxes to San Francisco. The original train depot remains.

By the turn of the 20th century, the Korbel brothers had acquired both fortune and international respect. But in 1919, they got spooked by Prohibition and sold their winemaking interest to cousins, who, in turn, let the business go to one Adolf Heck in 1954. Heck's son Gary took over the business in 1974. Their sparkling wine has often been used at White House dinners and presidential inaugurations, from President Ronald Reagan's 1985 inauguration to President Joe Biden's in 2021.

The 2,000-acre Korbel estate lies along the Russian River, and a visit to the garden here is a breathtaking encounter. Surrounded by towering old redwood trees, the garden is located on the hilly terrain. The tour starts at the original farmhouse that the Korbel brothers shared. The antique rose gardens, which include more than 250 varieties of old roses are all framed by box hedges and more than 1,000 varieties of other flowers, including pincushion plants, agapanthus, irises, and dahlias. Walking up the winding paths, you'll find 30-foot-tall climbing hydrangeas. Also look for a 130-year-old climbing Lamarque rose, with white petals and a beautiful fragrance, a gift to the Korbel family from horticulturist Luther Burbank.

Address 13250 River Road, Guerneville, CA 95446, +1 (707) 824-7000, www.korbel.com |
Getting there By car, from US-101, take exit 494 onto River Road and continue 13 miles
to the destination. | Hours Garden tours Apr–Oct, see website for schedule | Tip If you are
a beer lover, stop at Stumptown Brewery one mile away in Guerneville (15045 River Road,
Guerneville, www.stumptown.com).

64 Lachryma Montis

General Vallejo's estate

General Mariano Guadalupe Vallejo will always be remembered by historians for his various political identities, particularly his work to transfer Alta California from Mexico to the United States. He was a daring politician, a technocrat of the day, and a cagey diplomat, who learned to survive the endless intrigues of the mid-to-late 1800s in Northern California. Vallejo and his wife Doña Francisca Benicia Carrillo de Vallejo were also formidable entertainers. They were also known for their regard for local Indigenous tribes.

For a time, Vallejo was an extremely wealthy man, who owned two estates, one a *rancho* in Petaluma. The other was built in Sonoma on 20 acres in 1851 and founded on a free-flowing spring that eventually included a reservoir surrounded by an arbor covered in vines. The Indigenous name for the spring was "Crying Mountain," which inspired Vallejo, an unusually erudite man who spoke Latin, to christen the property *Lachryma Montis* (Mountain Tear). His two-story, wood-frame, gothic Victorian-style house included prefabricated sides imported from Europe. The property features fountains, gardens, and several outbuildings, including the hermitage where one of his sons, Napoleon Vallejo, an avid naturalist, lived with many pets, including 2 monkeys, a parrot, 14 dogs, and several cats.

Vallejo also built a small gazebo known as El Delirio. It was soon altered as a small office, where Vallejo found time to rewrite his five-volume history of California, *La Historia de California*. By the end of his life, General Vallejo had lost nearly everything except his reputation for graciousness and generosity.

The Vallejos lived here for 35 years, and today you can take a self-guided tour that leads you through all the rooms, which have been carefully restored. You'll feel as if you arrived just after the family stepped out for the afternoon in the 1870s.

Address 363 3rd Street W, Sonoma, CA 95476, +1 (707) 938-9559, www.sonomaparks.org/
location/general-vallejos-home | Getting there By car, from CA-121/Arnold Avenue in
Sonoma, take Petaluma Avenue E, turn right onto Riverside Drive to W Napa Street, and
turn left onto 3rd Street. | Hours Daily 10am–5pm | Tip Take a three-mile hike over a trail
originally used as hunting territory by native Americans to Sonoma Overlook and enjoy the
view of the valley (198 1st Street W, www.sonomaecologycenter.org/sonoma-overlook-trail).

65 Lisa Kristine Fine Art Gallery

A humanitarian photographer's view

At the Sonoma Plaza Mercato Building, you'll find an unexpected revelation: the Lisa Kristine Fine Art Gallery, filled with the most extraordinary images. The photographs in intense color are accompanied by narratives about the place and people. They are at once beautiful and often unnerving. The artist is best known for her portraits focused on victims of slavery and human trafficking. Such is the eye of this world-renowned "humanitarian photographer," who is also an activist and educator.

Kristine has won several major awards, including a Lucie Humanitarian Award in 2013. David Clarke, the one-time head of photography for Tate Modern, praised her work as a "testament to truth." She takes pictures of the otherwise invisible lives of Indigenous peoples and disappearing cultures. Her goal is simply to capture images and do it meticulously and always with great respect and intimate connection to the landscape and its people. Her images convey a truth about humanity and a wrong that needs to be addressed.

Kristine is guided by simple curiosity. "In other words," she says, "the people that I'm photographing, they're not my subjects. They're really my mentors. What interests me in photographing people is discovering their authenticity, dignity, intimacy; and perhaps, above all, signs of a life that has been truly lived. I've always felt the difference between living and letting time idly pass. I'm drawn to that sense of a pillar at one's core. No matter how dire, or difficult, or consequential a person's harsh environment may be – think of slavery – what I'm drawn to is their strength and dignity. I'm drawn to that part of them that is like an eternal flame."

Take your time when you visit the Lisa Kristine Gallery and expect to be moved by beautiful photos.

Address 452 1st Street E, Sonoma, CA 95476, +1 (707) 938-3860, www.lisakristine.com |
Getting there By car, take CA-12/Broadway to Sonoma Plaza, turn right onto E Napa
Street. and left onto 1st Street E. | Hours Thu noon–4pm, Fri & Sat 11am–6pm, Sun &
Mon 11am–4pm | Tip The Arts Guild of Sonoma is the oldest continuously operating
artists' collective in California and showcases the work of local artists (140 E Napa Street,
Sonoma, www.artsguildofsonoma.org).

66 The Lucky Mojo Curio Co.
That hoodoo that you do so well

Forestville lies a few miles northwest of Santa Rosa, off Route 116. A village of three thousand residents, it's a long-time bohemian capital and refuge from the humdrum. Consider, for example, the town's occult shop, the Lucky Mojo Curio Co.

This shop, though well known locally, is not easy to find. (The secret is an unmarked road.) But eventually the place reveals itself, and the first sign of something odd may be at ankle level. As you walk up to the shop, below bushes and around a runaway garden, there's a whole Swiftian world of towns, Lionel trains, and cars. Welcome to the mind of catherine yronwode, who styles her name in lowercase. She is, among other things, an astrologist, psychic reader, Hoodoo authority, mistress of the fantastic, folk magic author, graphic artist, and a comic book creator and publisher.

Lucky Mojo Curio Co. is open 365 days a year. The occult shop is filled with home-made hoodoo oils, incense, powders, and "spell kits." Herbs, from A to Z, are grown on the property. You get free tips on herbal spell-crafting. You'll notice the collection of minerals and roots, along with amulets, talismans, arrowheads, and charmstones. There's also a library of occult books, including yronwode's *Hoodoo in Theory and Practice*, a meditation on conjure craft, how to make "mojo bags," lay tricks, and otherwise live in the world of African American traditions of folk magic.

Among the larger peculiarities in the shop, you'll find a skeleton named Lefty and a six-foot-tall wizard with a crystal ball. The shop's website is a popular souk filled with links to user fora on subjects like karezza, neo-tantra, and sacred sexuality.

The Missionary Independent Spiritual Church of Forestville, which claims to be "one of the smallest churches in the world," is located in front of Lucky Mojo Curio Co. and offers a daily candle service to the public.

Address 6632 Covey Road, Forestville, CA 95436, +1 (707) 887-1521, www.luckymojo.com | Getting there By car, from US-101, take exit 494 onto River Road west, continue seven miles and turn left onto Trenton Road and left onto Covey Road. | Hours Daily 9am–5pm | Tip To satisfy your hunger, you must stop and try some of the delicious breads at Nightingale Breads (6665 Front Street, www.nightingalebreads.com).

67 __ Luther Burbank Home & Gardens

A living monument to a plant luminary

The grounds of the Luther Burbank Home and Gardens include plant beds, a museum, a greenhouse, and the house where Luther Burbank (1849–1926) lived with his second wife Elizabeth Waters. Burbank was a botanist who thought about links between plant evolution and human evolution. He was a renaissance man, good natured and confident. He was an amateur scientist, a humanist, a futurist in the context of agricultural sustainability, a would-be educator, and altogether a close student of the human condition.

Henry Ford, Helen Keller, and Thomas Edison met Burbank at his gardens in Santa Rosa. Frida Kahlo and Diego Riviera paid a visit to his home. They were all inspired by Burbank's life and philosophy. Rivera depicted him as the symbol of fertile California agriculture in the Pacific Stock Exchange mural *Allegory of California*. Kahlo painted him as a hybrid with his human upper body and a tree bottom, the work that started her favorite theme, "the fertilization of life by death."

Burbank brought to life some 800 varieties of plants and is best known for creating the Shasta daisy, the Flaming gold nectarine, and the freestone peach, as well as plum varieties known as the plumcot, the Santa Rosa, and the Wickson. He helped create the spineless cactus and the Russet Burbank potato, developed to counter the disastrous effects of the Great Hunger, the blight that began in 1845 in western and southern Ireland and lasted nearly a decade.

"What a joy life is," noted Burbank in a 1926 speech, the year he died, "when you have made a close working partnership with Nature, helping her to produce for the benefit of mankind new forms – new food for all the world's untold millions for all time to come." Burbank is buried in the memorial area under a cedar of Lebanon tree.

Address 204 Santa Rosa Avenue, Santa Rosa, CA 95404, +1 (707) 524-5445, www.lutherburbank.org, burbankhome@lutherburbank.org | Getting there By car, from US-101, take exit 488A and turn left onto Santa Rosa Avenue. | Hours Daily 8am–dusk | Tip Visit Gold Ridge Experimental Farm in Sebastopol, the three-acre farm established by Luther Burbank in 1885 where he conducted his large-scale plant experiments (7777 Bodega Avenue, Sebastopol, www.wschs.org).

68 Mcevoy Ranch

Behind the world's finest extra virgin olive oil

Before she turned to producing extra virgin olive oil in Petaluma in 1990, Nan Tucker McEvoy (1919–2015) had done many things. She grew up after World War I during the age of cotillions. Her grandfather was M. H. de Young, who founded what would become the San Francisco Chronicle in 1865. McEvoy herself worked as a reporter for the paper in the 1940s and then in 1981 became chairwoman of the Chronicle's parent company. She was ever a good liberal. In her obituary, Chronicle writer Sam Whiting wrote that although "she lived her entire life amid great wealth, she never took to the leisure class or the conservative line that was expected."

Early on, she worked as an executive recruiter for the Peace Corps and later founded an abortion clinic for low-income women in Washington, DC, where she became a close friend of Katherine Graham, publisher of the *Washington Post*. McEvoy was tall, formidable, gregarious, and unflappable. She was forever defying the odds and the status quo.

In the late 1980s, McEvoy bought 550 acres in Petaluma and eventually planted 18,000 trees bearing Tuscan olives. She studied the science of agriculture. She also benefited from the microclimate characteristic of the Petaluma Gap. That's a geographic area extending from the coast to San Pablo Bay. Warm air rises off the land, allowing cold, moist air, along with wind and fog, to move in underneath. The effect has become legendary for the McEvoy Ranch, whose olives have been rated among the best in the world by magazines like *Saveur* and *Consumer Reports*.

In addition to the olive trees and vineyards on the ranch, you'll come across the fantasy-like Chinese Pavilion with its striking interior brimming with pendant lanterns and a mosaic stone floor. You'll also enjoy seeing an exceptional art collection, the main house, and a unique Victorian building with a painted cabinet by McEvoy's friend Wayne Thiebaud.

Address 5935 Red Hill Road, Petaluma, CA 94952, +1 (707) 778-2307, www.mcevoyranch.com | Getting there By car, from US-101, take exit 467 and turn onto S San Antonio Road northwest, then left onto San Antonio Road, and left onto D Street to Red Hill Road. | Hours Daily 11am–5pm by appointment | Tip For birdwatching, stop at Shollenberger Park, where you'll spot many birds and other wildlife throughout 165 acres of wetlands (1400 Cader Lane, Petaluma, www.cityofpetaluma.org/shollenberger-park).

69 Mission San Francisco Solano de Sonoma

The last Franciscan mission

By the early 1800s, the Spanish Church had established its string of missions between San Diego and Sonoma. The missions were positioned about 30 miles apart, or roughly a day's ride. The last and furthest north was Mission San Francisco Solano, founded in the town of Sonoma on July 4th, 1823 by Spanish-born Father José Altimira. This mission was defending the area from a growing Russian presence in the Northwest at Fort Point. It's all part of the mission exhibit on the northeast corner of the Sonoma town plaza.

Ten years later, the mission was largely self-sufficient and included a rectory with 37 rooms, a large adobe church, a storehouse, and shops for training craftsmen, artisans, and farmers. Altimira himself was well known for his bad temper and for not sharing a bountiful harvest. In 1826 Native Americans attacked the mission, and he ran away.

The mission was designed around a large quadrangle. Beyond the perimeter were vineyards, orchards, gardens, and housing for soldiers. There was a jail, a cemetery, an infirmary, and an area for Native American families, which included so-called "neophytes," or budding Christians. An accounting of the Mission's 10th year in 1832 recorded 127 baptisms, 34 marriages, 70 deaths, 900 horses, and 996 neophytes. But in 1835, the Mexican government secularized the missions, and by 1839, this one had fallen into ruin. It was partially restored in 1913. Then, in 1841 General Vallejo had a new, simple chapel constructed alongside the original mission quadrangle.

On the west side of the mission is a commemorative granite wall with names of over 800 Native American people, including 200 children, who died working at the mission. The inscriptions on the memorial wall, dedicated in 1999, reflect their Christian names.

Address 114 E Spain Street, Sonoma, CA 95476, +1 (707) 938-9560, www.sonomaparks.org/location/mission-san-francisco-solano, parkinfo@sonomaparks.org | Getting there By car, take CA-12/Broadway to Sonoma Plaza, turn right onto E Napa Street, left onto 1st Street E, and right onto East Spain Street. | Hours Daily 10am–5pm | Tip Stop by Sonoma Valley Museum of Art, a vibrant museum of modern and contemporary art (551 Broadway, Sonoma, www.svma.org).

70__Moon House
The art of an archeologist

And then you come to Moon House, as obscure, unexpected, and dazzling a place as you'll find. The iron gate to the Moon House is locked, but you can reserve a tour. From the gate through the trees, it gives the impression of an Incan temple ruin. In fact, it's a 5,000-square-foot antiquarium filled with fascinating objects. It's also an art gallery, residence, and studio. And it's all the mind of Douglas Fenn Wilson, a tall, affable man, who will come to open the door and take you on a tour.

Wilson is the consummate artist. All the fixtures and finishes in the house, from countertops to the friezes to the fragments excavated from an ancient city, were designed and fabricated by Wilson. Nonprofits host galas here. When it's all dressed up in candles, you couldn't imagine a more exciting and enticing place to entertain.

There's a wonderful conceit with all this, which is that Wilson has cast the house and everything you see as part of a fictional narrative to give his archaeology a context. The story is about the house as if it were built in 1917 by a great uncle Augustus Fenn and destroyed by a mudslide in 1937. Excerpts from the story are framed on the wall and cast as archeological finds. Wilson is forever exploring the intersections of past and present in sculptures, paintings, novels and short stories, and architecture. Wilson's own paintings are distinguished by a layered effect, an excavation that suggests you're seeing something unburied, revealed, perhaps a truth forgotten.

He once wrote, "I come from a point of view of one standing apart from the present – in some imagined future looking back at the still frames of my life – moments of captured and remembered beauty – their pasts dissolving into eroded structure, into archeology, the future peeled away and still peeling until all that's left is a fabulous glimpse of a present that was."

Address 13785 Arnold Drive, Glen Ellen, CA 95442, www.moonhouseant.com | Getting there By car, from Sonoma, take Arnold Drive N to Glen Ellen. | Hours Viewable from the outside only | Tip Across the street you'll find the Les Pascals bakery, known for its quiches and delicious pastries (13758 Arnold Drive, Glen Ellen, www.lespascalspatisserie.com).

71 Mountain Cemetery

Where Sonoma history is laid to rest

Set on roughly 80 acres of terraces in among the moss-coated oaks is Sonoma's Mountain Cemetery, a vivid reflection of Sonoma's heritage and the area's general wealth. The earliest burials are from the 1840s, but city officials don't know how many people are buried here. One estimate puts that number "in the rough hundreds." The details of when the site was chosen and how the town acquired it aren't known either. Unfortunately, the cemetery has fallen on hard times in recent years because, even with volunteers, the annual cost sometimes runs to several hundred thousand dollars.

You can pick up a free walking-tour brochure at the Sonoma Overlook Trail kiosk or download it from the website. Look for famous residents buried here, including William Smith, the only known Revolutionary War veteran buried in the State of California, and John McCracken, one of the first pioneers to settle in Sonoma. And you'll find the grave of Henry Boyes (1844–1919), who arrived from England in 1888 and discovered a hot spring with 112-degree water. He established a popular resort for vacationers from San Francisco. Other graves hold the remains of famous local families, including that of Samuele Sebastiani (1874–1944), founder of historic Sebastiani Winery established in 1904 in the town of Sonoma.

There's also the grave of a Native American child. The identity is unclear and raises the question of why this child was not buried a half mile away with the 900 Native people in unmarked graves near Mission San Francisco Solano. Finally, there is the immaculate grave of General Mariano Vallejo and his wife Francisca Benicia Carrillo. He was a wealthy landowner, the founder of Sonoma, a dexterous diplomat who spoke Latin and French as well as Spanish, and an early Californian Thomas Jefferson. Before the general sold it off, the cemetery ground belonged to him.

Address 90 1st Street W, Sonoma, CA 95476, +1 (707) 933-2218, www.sonomacity.org/mountain-cemetery | Getting there By car, take CA-12/Broadway to Sonoma Plaza, turn left onto W Napa Street, and right onto 1st Street W. | Hours Daily 8am–5pm | Tip The nearby Sonoma Depot Museum focuses on the history of the Sonoma Railroad (270 1st Street W, www.depotparkmuseum.org).

72 Mystic Theater & Music Hall

Where American Graffiti and music meet

The Mystic Theater in downtown Petaluma last showed feature films in 1988, marking the end of an era that began in 1912, when the theater opened through various incarnations under different names and owners. It was originally the Mystic, then the State, the Plaza, the Palace, and McNear's Mystic Theater & Music Hall since 1992.

Over the years the now 500-seat theater has offered Vaudeville, first-run feature films, pornography, and some of the great names in popular music, including Van Morrison, Stephen Marley, Carlos Santana, and Snoop Dogg. In 1972, George Lucas used the front of the then State Theater in *American Graffiti*. In the film, the theater marquee read "Dementia 13," one of Lucas's first films.

These days, the Mystic program features only live music "up close and loud," with some exceptions, including Micro Mania Midget Wrestling, a wildly popular event that first took off in 2000 in the upper Midwest. It features WWE wrestlers, both men and women, under five feet tall. As for music, the Mystic presents long-time local favorites, such as Zepparella, an all-female Led Zeppelin tribute band; Mordred, a funk metal/thrash metal band, whose strongest fanbase is in Germany; and Rising Appalachia, an American folk music band starring two instrumentalist sisters.

It was in 1886 that John A. McNear built what is now McNear's Saloon and Dining House. The theater was built next door in 1911. Now both buildings are regarded as one, the McNear Building. At the turn of the 20th century, McNear was already Petaluma's beloved patriarch, a Midas who, along with his son, turned one opportunity after another into wealth, from shipping and utilities, to banking, real estate, and poultry. Today, the building is home to more than 50 small businesses.

Address 23 Petaluma Boulevard N, Petaluma, CA 94952, +1 (707) 775-6048, mystictheatre.com, mysticpetaluma@gmail.com | Getting there By car, from US-101, take exit 474 onto E Washington Street towards downtown Petaluma and turn left onto Petaluma Boulevard N. | Hours See website for event schedule | Tip You must try the poached pear almond croissant and other sweet and savory Italian pastries at Stellina Pronto (23 Kentucky Street, Petaluma, www.stellinapronto.com).

73 Native Riders
A flourishing, modern trading post

In recent centuries, even millennia, at least three large Native American tribes have lived in and around Sonoma, Napa, and Mendocino Counties. The Pomo people lived north of Ft. Bragg, and the "central" Wappo lived between Santa Rosa and Healdsburg, at the Northern end of the Russian River Valley. And the Miwok people lived around Bodega Bay and then east in what would become Petaluma and Sonoma.

Naturally, territories overlapped, expanded, or contracted. The history these tribes hold in common is that casually forgotten trail of humiliation, illness, displacement, and death at the hands of European and American colonizers.

Nevertheless, Native American cultures survive and even flourish in Northern California. Native Riders is one of a handful of community centers and stores and offers an extraordinary collection of finely crafted leather and feather goods, and memorabilia.

Store owner Kerry Mitchell, an accomplished entrepreneur with Comanche roots, otherwise known as Lone Eagle, opened his first store in Southern California in 1971. He has gone on to become an expert leather craftsman and has won numerous awards for his work. These days, he specializes in designs for horse shows, parades, pow wows, and festivals. His costumes have appeared in such films as *Dances With Wolves* and *Windwalker*. Clint Eastwood, Ann Margaret, and Cher, among many other actors, own his designs.

The Native Riders store is small and carefully laid out. A sampling of popular items includes exotic dream catchers, wooden sculptures, wall hangings, fresh Canadian sweetgrass, jewelry, belts, braids, antler peace pipes, red fox tails, sacred incense smudge kits, deerskin baby moccasins, and gorgeous large peacock feathers. Mitchell's work appears at festivals such as Burning Spear, the Kate Wolf Memorial Festival, Monterey Reggae Fest, and Gaia Fest.

Address 5600 Gravenstein Highway S, Sebastopol, CA 95472, +1 (707) 829-8544, www.sonomacounty.com/shopping/native-riders | Getting there By car, from US-101, take exit 481B onto CA-116/Gravenstein Highway N towards Sebastopol. | Hours Tue – Sun 9am – 6pm | Tip The Museum of the American Indian in Novato features historical pieces and contemporary Native American arts (2200 Novato Boulevard, Novato, www.marinindian.com).

74 Northwood Golf Course
Links to the ethereal

Among the world's great golf course architects was Alister Mackenzie (1870–1934). Born in Yorkshire with Scots blood, he became a surgeon and went off to the Boer War. He came back fascinated by the nature of camouflage, which led him to the art of combining natural and synthetic features on a golf course. Though not a notable player himself, he became a master of the greens. He designed more than 50 courses around the world, including the Augusta National Golf Club in Georgia and the Cypress Point Club in Monterey, California. He also laid out the Pasatiempo Golf Course in Santa Cruz, where he died in his home on the sixth hole.

Dr. MacKenzie, with bushy eyebrows and moustache, believed in 13 principles of sound design. They were laid out in his book, *The Spirit of St. Andrews.* "There should be a complete absence of the annoyance caused by the necessity of searching for lost balls," he wrote. "The course should be so interesting that even the scratch man is stimulated to improve his game in attempting shots he has hitherto been unable to play." He continued, "The course should have such a natural appearance that a stranger is unable to distinguish the course from nature itself."

In 1928, the famous Bohemian Club in San Francisco commissioned Dr. MacKenzie to create a 2,893-yard, 9-hole course for their members to have a place to golf during the summer encampment. It's called Northwood, and it's located just across the river from the Bohemian grounds. It runs along the Russian River near Monte Rio, a few miles west of Guerneville. The course is among the most beautiful courses in the world, with long narrow greens, and here you are as though in a cathedral of redwoods, following the mind of a designer whose abiding interest is to ensure that even the highest par player has a good time. It's open to the public most of the year.

Address 19400 Highway 116, Monte Rio, CA 95462, +1 (707) 865-1116, www.northwoodgolf.com | Getting there By car, from US-101, take exit 494 onto River Road and continue 18 miles to the destination. | Hours See website for seasonal hours | Tip You'll also enjoy a golf course with a view of the Pacific Ocean at The Links at Bodega Harbour (21301 Heron Drive, Bodega Bay, www.bodegaharbourgolf.com).

75__ The Occidental Arts & Ecology Center
The beauty of the cutting edge

Just north of Occidental lies the Occidental Arts & Ecology Center (OAEC), an 80-acre intentional community and working farm founded in 1994. Its charter is to be an advocacy organization and develop strategies for "regional-scale community resilience and the restoration of biological and cultural diversity."

Specific programs address permaculture design and wildlife restoration. There's also a garden biodiversity program, featuring a seed bank with more than 3,000 varieties of open-pollinated annuals and over 1,000 varieties of medicinal perennials. In addition, the center sponsors the WATER Institute, which is focused on conservation hydrology and the need to choose rehydration over dehydration.

While the center is not open to walk-ins, you can make a reservation to participate in various activities, including Sunday tours, garden volunteer days, and workshops and courses on such topics as community resilience and restoration. If you come to these events, you can have lunch too, which is particularly sumptuous. The center is designed for organizational retreats and conferences, with accommodations, including sleeping quarters, hot tub, and hiking. The people who live and work here are congenial and very knowledgeable about the workings of an intentional community. The center extends this invitation: "When visitors come to the Occidental Arts & Ecology Center, they are not showing up to a hotel or conference center. They come as honored guests in our home."

OAEC's Mother Garden Nursery just up on the road is open on the weekends from April through October. Among mostly perennials and drought-tolerant plants, you can find plants that are edible, medicinal, or used for dye making, all 100% organic. The staff is very welcoming and happy to share their knowledge of plants.

Address 15290 Coleman Valley Road, Occidental, CA 95465, +1 (707) 847-1557, www.oaec.org, oaec@oaec.org | Getting there By car, from US-101, take exit 488B onto CA-12 W towards Sebastopol. Turn right onto Fulton Road, left onto Occidental Road, right onto Green Hill Road, and left onto Graton Road. Turn left onto Bohemian Highway and then right onto Coleman Valley Road. | Hours OAEC: See website for events, tours, and courses; Mother Garden Nursery: Apr–Oct Sat & Sun 10am–5pm | Tip Stop by Hand Goods, a gallery featuring handcrafted goods from pottery to jewelry and home goods (3627 Main Street, Occidental, www.handgoodsoccidental.com).

76 __ Oliver Ranch
Art born among the oaks

Oliver Ranch is a sculpture park, located on 100 acres, among rolling hills sprinkled with native oaks. The artists who are invited to come here must live on the ranch and experience the land. The result is born there on the spot. And the art stays, never to be moved, never to be sold.

It all started in 1985 with Steve and Nancy Oliver's commitment to art and sharing their collection with others. They bought the ranch in 1981 to raise sheep. Seeking a more individual way of engaging with artists, they decided to invite artist Judy Shea to create the first site-specific work for their property. Today, there are 18 art installations. They each tell a story, set against the rhythm of the trees and hills around them. And, like the oaks and the hills, they make you feel they have been there for centuries, not a mere 30 years or so.

There is Ann Hamilton's Tower, where dance, poetry, theater, and music performances take place. The Tower, with a double-helix staircase inside, goes almost as far into the earth as it does into the air. It's open to the sky at the top, with a water cistern at the base. And there is Roger Barry's steel bridge *Darwin*. On the summer and winter solstices, the shadow cast on the ground is only from its respective arch. On the spring and autumnal equinoxes, the shadow cast is exactly split by a strip of light that comes down through the center of the arch. The accuracy of this shadow split by the light is within one millimeter.

On a 2.5-mile hike through the hills, you see other impressive sculptures by 20 award-winning and world famous artists: Martin Puryear, Richard Serra, Terry Allen, Ellen Driscoll, Bill Fontana, Kristin Jones, Andrew Ginzel, Andy Goldsworthy, Dennis Leon, Jim Melchert, Fred Sandback, Judith Shea, Robert Stackhouse, Ursula Von Rydingsvard, Miroslaw Balka, Doug Hall, Bruce Nauman, David Rabinowitch, and Jim Jennings.

Address 22205 River Road, Geyserville, CA 9544, +1 (707) 857-3975, www.oliverranchfoundation.org | Getting there By car, from US-101, take exit 510 and turn right onto Geyserville Avenue, then left onto CA-128 and left onto River Road. | Hours See website for tour schedules | Tip The Lake Sonoma Visitor Center and Fish Hatchery features natural and early history exhibits focusing on the Pomo people of Dry Creek Valley (3333 Skaggs Springs Road, Geyserville).

77 — Pacific Coast Air Museum
Phantom flyers from the past

Among the most fearsome warplanes ever built was the F-4 Phantom. More than 5,000 rolled out of the MacDonald Douglas factory in the late 1950s and early 60s. Colonel Charles DeBellevue, a Phantom pilot, once noted, "The F-4 Phantom was the last plane that looked like it was made to kill somebody. It had a reputation of being a clumsy bruiser reliant on brute engine power and obsolete weapons technology." The two-seater jet was used extensively during the Vietnam War, when 761 F-4s were lost from all services, and mostly to ground fire. It gave as good as it got and earned the nickname "The World's Leading Distributor of MiG Parts." Advanced versions are still used by some countries.

The Phantom is one of about two dozen aircraft exhibits at the Pacific Coast Air Museum, tucked away in a corner of the Charles M. Schulz-Sonoma County Airport, a few miles north of Santa Rosa. The mostly military aircraft represent the evolution of design from the 1950s until now. Visitors can sit in the cockpit of some aircraft. Exhibits include the F-15 Eagle that first responded to the attack on the World Trade Center on 9/11. The museum features dioramas, equipment, photographs and memorabilia, and an original World War II-era fabrication shop.

Try out a 3D Virtual Reality Flight Simulator. A curator gets you up and running with a brief training for your 20-minute "flight." Advanced simulation pilots can participate in dog fights and refueling exercises. There are at least 16 flight programs from which to choose. You can fly a World War I Sopwith Camel, the famous British fighter introduced to the Western front in 1917; a P-51 Mustang, which ruled the skies of Europe at the end of World War II; or an F/A-18 Hornet, an engineering marvel known for survivability. There's no program for Phantoms, but there is one for an AV-8B Harrier Jump Jet, which can take off vertically.

Address 1 Air Museum Way, Santa Rosa, CA 95403, +1 (707) 575-7900,
www.pacificcoastairmuseum.org, admin@pacificcoastairmuseum.org | Getting there By
car, rom US-101, take exit 495 onto Airport Boulevard towards the airport, turn left onto
N Laughlin Road, and turn right onto Becker Boulevard. | Hours Wed–Sun 10am–4pm |
Tip Go on an African safari at Safari West and encounter a wide range of animals,
including giraffes, antelopes, and a rhinoceros (3115 Porter Creek Road, Santa Rosa,
www.safariwest.com).

78 Petaluma Collective Antique Mall
A world of military memorabilia and antiques

"Militaria" is a term coined in 1964, coincidentally the year the Gulf of Tonkin Resolution was passed, marking the US' official entrance into the Vietnam War. The word refers to the vast world of military memorabilia collections, usually weapons and uniforms, but also odd bits of equipment, a tachometer for example, as well as medals and ephemera, such as badges, diaries, portraits, press releases, and operating manuals – in sum, the paraphernalia of war.

The Petaluma Collective Antique & Militaria Mall, hosts dozens of stalls where you can buy, sell, or trade these objects, or simply peruse or strike up a conversation with the other like-minded antique hunters and dealers. It's a souk, where you can also find ceramics, glass, old photos, and vintage records. But most of the stalls feature military antiques, and it's said that this spot is one of the largest sources in the Bay Area. The venue has a vast variety of different products sorted into categories, such as antique firearms, aviation-related items, German World War II military artifacts, and more.

Collections are constantly changing here. German items might include a reproduction of a Luftwaffe paratrooper's gravity knife, a reproduction of an 88mm fuse, and German dog tags and badges. Other collections include a 15th Corps badge from the Civil War, a Cold War-era emergency signal mirror, a World War II-era mess kit, a pair of women's trousers, and *Life* magazines. One of the oldest items is a US musket Model 1795 dating to 1826, the first flintlock musket the government produced after the Revolutionary War.

Look for a sign that reads, "To avoid future totalitarian governments, it is important to remember the past. The preservation of these items helps to keep the memory of those horrors alive."

Address 300 Petaluma Boulevard N, Petaluma, CA 94952 , +1 (707) 763-2220,
www.militaryantiquesmuseum.com, warguys@sonic.net | Getting there By car, from
US-101, take exit 474 onto E Washington Street towards downtown Petaluma and
turn right onto Petaluma Boulevard N. | Hours Daily 10am–5:30pm | Tip Check out
the bronze armwrestling statue of two men in competitive grapple. Petaluma used to be
an armwrestling capital. Every October, Petaluma hosted the World Wrist Wrestling
Championship, with over 300 competitors (423 E Washington Street, Petaluma).

79__Petaluma Seed Bank
Because dire is here

As climate change rates accelerate, along with a gathering dread of food scarcity because of war or economic calamity, the Seed Saver Movement has become increasingly popular. It started in the 1980s in India. Today, the largest seed bank in the world is The Millennium Seed Bank Partnership, located in a nuclear bomb-proof vault in a London suburb.

In the US, one of the larger seed banks is the Baker Creek Heirloom Seed Company, a farm and long-term seed savings and storage organization in Mansfield, Missouri. The founder Jere Gettle started the company in 1998 when he was 17. In 2009 they opened a retail store in the historic district of downtown Petaluma. The store was originally in an old bank, hence the reference to a bank. Nevertheless, all storage is in Missouri. Baker Creek publishes an annual *Whole Seed Catalog* with more than 1,275 kinds of seeds; the Petaluma store has them all, including certified local favorites, such as garlic and herbs from Marin and Sonoma. A staff favorite is Dad's Sunset tomatoes, along with certified organic seed potatoes in the spring, including the almost extinct Bodega Red.

The Petaluma store offers a "Homesteading Seed Collection," designed for "off-grid" gardeners. The seeds include vegetables, herbs, flowers, and grains, and last four to 10 years. The collection also has a Clyde's Garden Planner slide chart, five clay desiccant packs, 35 full-sized packs of heirloom non-GMO seeds, an herb-specific growing sheet, and general information on self-sustaining food production.

Baker Creek provides free seeds to hundreds of communities and educational groups each year and is dedicated to the notion that farmers, gardeners, and communities "have the right to save their own seeds, and so preserve seed diversity and food security in an age of corporate agriculture and patented, hybridized or genetically modified seeds."

Address 110 Petaluma Boulevard N, Petaluma, CA 94952, +1 (707) 773-1336,
www.rareseeds.com/petaluma-seed-bank, seeds@rareseeds.com | Getting there By car,
from US-101, take exit 474 onto E Washington Street towards downtown Petaluma and
turn left onto Petaluma Boulevard N. | Hours Sun–Thu 10am–4pm | Tip For more
gardening supplies, you can visit Harmony Farm Supply and Nursery (5400 Old Redwood
Highway N, Penngrove, www.harmonyfarm.com).

80 Petaluma Wildlife & Natural Science Museum

The nation's largest student-run enterprise of its kind

In 1989, a close group of teachers, students, and administrators at Petaluma High School created what has become the country's largest student-run natural history museum. The site grew out of an old bus garage that was transformed into a 9,000-square-foot museum featuring fabulous, high-quality dioramas – the taxidermy is stunning – along with quarters for about 40 live animals and various exhibits. Ron Head, the museum's founder, imagined a place where high school students could develop leadership and management skills while also studying natural history and the care required to sustain live animals in a controlled environment.

Philip Tacata directs the school's museum program today. This is a short excerpt from his introduction to its pedagogy: "In order for your generation to correct the mistakes of those-before, you have to do exactly the opposite of what got us here: YOU HAVE TO GIVE… your time, your passion, and your dedication to rebuilding and restructuring a world decimated by decades of greed."

The seven-room museum, located at Petaluma High School, is open to the public on Saturdays only. Tours are given by high school students, who are knowledgeable, friendly, and well versed. You'll learn about such topics as animal adaptation, fossil history, biodiversity, and issues around poaching and conservation. Notable exhibits include an African savanna biome, with all the classic animals associated with Africa, from zebras to lions. There's a forestry exhibit, mineral collections, and a reptile room. There's also a North American room divided into various fauna zones. Of particular interest is "the cave," where you'll find a display of both troglobites and arthropods. Children will find these dioramas totally compelling.

Address 201 Fair Street, Petaluma, CA 94952, +1 (707) 778-4787,
www.petalumawildlifemuseum.org, info@petalumawildlifemuseum.com | Getting there
By car, from US-101, take exit 472 onto Lakeville Street towards downtown Petaluma.
Turn left onto D Street, right onto 10th Street, and continue onto Fair Street. | Hours Sat
11am–3pm | Tip Spring Lake's Environmental Discovery Center is another natural history
museum with hands-on exhibits, a tide pool with touchable sea creatures, Shelby the turtle,
and wildlife displays (393 Violetti Road, Santa Rosa, parks.sonomacounty.ca.gov/visit/
environmental-discovery-center).

81 Pond Farm

Marguerite Wildenhain's art colony

Peter Voulkos and Robert Arneson are among the many celebrated ceramicists in California art history. And then there is Marguerite Wildenhain (1896–1985), that wondrous craftswoman, teacher and artist, and one of the most important ceramicists of the midcentury American studio craft movement. Arneson once described Wildenhain as the "grand dame of ceramics."

She was born into an upper middle-class family in France and fell under the spell of the Bauhaus movement. Wildenhain became the first woman named a Master Potter during the interwar years in Europe and the first female master at the Bauhaus. She was Jewish and fled the Nazi occupation of Holland in 1940. She would find her way to a 140-acre experimental art colony near Guerneville. It was called Pond Farm. The school thrived for three years. Marguerite then bought the property and conducted her famous nine-week, intensive summer school for 15 to 20 promising artists over a 30-year period, in addition to producing her own work. She demanded all students spend seven hours a day at the wheel. The emphasis was not on technique, but rather, as she once put it, on "what you can convey."

When Wildenhain died in 1985, the farm was taken over by the State of California and became part of the Austin Creek State Recreation Area. The place is located in the hills above Armstrong Redwood forest, hidden in a lush and tranquil landscape. Wildenhain was known as a powerful protector of the land and nature. The ranch consists of her house, a barn made into a pottery studio, and a guesthouse with an eight-acre garden and landscape. The small, Bauhaus-style potters' kick-wheels are still in working condition. The property has been designated a "National Treasure" by the National Trust for Historic Preservation, and the plan is to preserve the barn and home and use the guesthouse for a writer-in-residence program.

Address 17000 Armstrong Woods Road, Guerneville, CA 95446, www.pondfarm.org, stewards@stewardscr.org | **Getting there** By car, from US-101, take exit 494 onto River Road, continue 15 miles, and then turn right onto Armstrong Woods Road. | **Hours** See website for tour schedule | **Tip** The Armstrong Visitor Center and Gift Shop offers exhibits about the park's natural and cultural history, and sells books about Marguerite Wildenhain (www.stewardscr.org/armstrong-redwoods-facilities-activities).

82 Potter School House
Nature's evil streak

The ever-droll, British-born film director Alfred Hitchcock shot many of his features in Northern California. He owned a vineyard and ranch in Scotts Valley, north of Santa Cruz. The local spots in his films include downtown Santa Rosa in *Shadow of a Doubt* (1943); Big Sur in *Suspicion* (1941); Carmel and various places in San Francisco in *Vertigo* (1958); and Bodega Bay and the smaller town of Bodega in *The Birds* (1963).

The schoolhouse used in *The Birds* would appear to be in Bodega Bay, but it's actually eleven miles inland in Bodega, the small town with a population of 220. The school was built in the 19th century, and the exterior was restored for the film. The place is now privately owned. The monkey bars that attracted an ominous crowd of crows, as Tippi Hedren sat oblivious to the danger just behind her, are gone. The white wooden church you see in the movie is just behind the schoolhouse. In 1953, 10 years before filming, Ansel Adams took the famous black-and-white photo of that same church, built in 1862.

Just across the road from the church, you'll find *The Birds* Museum, tucked away in a corner of the Bodega Country Store. It features paintings, photos, memorabilia, and other oddities related to the movie.

The Birds, which some have called an "animal revenge film," was based partly on a novel by Daphne Du Maurier, as well as two real life events. One occurred in 1960 in La Jolla, California, where hundreds of birds flew down a house chimney and laid waste to the interior. Another incident, which immediately drew Hitchcock's interest, took place in Santa Cruz in August 1961, when thousands of sooty shearwaters attacked cars and houses around Monterey Bay.

To guide his film, Hitchcock made "exact replicas" of everything in Bodega Bay and had every single man, woman, and child in the town photographed for the costume department.

Address 17110 Bodega Lane, Bodega, CA 94922 | Getting there By car, from US-101, take exit 479 onto W Railroad Avenue, turn right onto Stony Point Road, left onto Roblar Road, right onto Valley Ford Road, and right onto Bodega Highway to Bodega. | Hours Viewable from the outside only | Tip To see the work of the local artists, visit The Historic Town of Bodega Art Gallery, located in the original blacksmith shop from the 1850s (17255 Bodega Highway, www.bodegaartgallery.com).

83 The Pygmy Forest
Natural goth

They're called "pygmy forests," or "elfin forests." You find them in highland areas and on isolated coastal mountains around the world; the largest is in the Philippines. They also appear up and down the California coast, particularly in southern Mendocino and northern Sonoma County.

There were once as many as 30 of these extraordinary forests on the headlands here, but most were lost to development. Now two prevail: the Van Damme State Park in Mendocino and Salt Point State Park in Sonoma. Both stand on ancient marine terraces where sandy soil – perhaps up to one million years old – has accumulated atop impermeable layers of iron and sandstone. As a result, neither roots nor water can penetrate the hardpan, and so all growth becomes stunted. Consider a tree trunk with a diameter of a quarter of an inch with 80 growth rings.

The forests include Bishop and Bolander pine, as well as Mendocino cypress, which in a normal forest might grow to 100 feet. Here, the trees reach eye level, and so from time to time as you walk along, you have the odd sensation of being above the forest. You would expect to find a trove of animals, but other than frogs and lizards, all kinds of mice, a lone deer, and an occasional birdsong, there is hardly any sign of traditional habitat. Look for diminutive plants too, such as Mount Hood pussypaws and Bird's-foot trefoil.

Salt Point Park, which lies on both sides of Route 1, extends over 6,000 acres, with 20 miles of hiking trails. Camping is permitted. The terrain is odd to be sure, much different from the redwood groves nearby. But this is the revelation. You come here to contemplate the whole "ecological staircase," not just the terrain. Salt Point is named after the crystals lodged in the rocky outcroppings. The Kashaya Pomo collected salt here for many years. In the 1850s, sandstone quarried here was used to pave the streets of San Francisco.

Address 25050 Highway 1, Jenner, CA 95450, www.parks.ca.gov | Getting there By car, from US-101, take exit 494 onto River Road, continue 27 miles, and turn right onto CA-1. Continue another 20 miles to the destination. | Hours Daily dawn–dusk | Tip It's a short hike to the sandy Stump Beach Cove with a nice picnic area (25050 Highway 1, Jenner, www.californiabeaches.com/beach/stump-beach-cove).

84 Rainbow Cattle Company
Where wood was gold

Guerneville was originally a lumber town, and after the 1906 earthquake shook and burned San Francisco to the ground, the place felt the equivalent of a gold rush. At the same time, the town became a playground for the wealthy from the city. In the late 1970s, gay entrepreneurs saw vacation housing opportunities for the LGBTQIA+ community. For a time, the town became a "gay mecca" that attracted the likes of The Fabulous Sylvester, a singer who specialized in disco and soul, and the Sisters of Perpetual Indulgence, the renowned drag queens, whose local chapter in Guerneville still performs and also hosts monthly bingo games. Then the AIDS epidemic struck in the 1980s, and the place dimmed and grew quiet.

These days Guerneville, 12 miles from the coast, still holds on to its gay vibe, although lately it has become increasingly diverse with a mix of hippies, retirees, crafters, refugees from Silicon Valley, vintners, and painters, who together form a culture both traditional and quirky.

"Basically, it's crowds of very hairy men," Bobby Frederick will tell you. He owns one of the original gay bars, the Rainbow Cattle Company, where not much has changed over the years, including the Madonna videos playing on the overhead monitors. Tuesday is Give Back Night, when local nonprofits gather at the bar to raise money – the Fire Department one night, Animal Rescue another. Characters who show up include California Mermaid Vira Burgerman. She's a local do-gooder and hairdresser, "tail and all."

Since the pandemic, the town has retrieved some of its swagger. The party feeling is coming back; old animosities have subsided. The annual Sonoma County Pride Parade and Celebration is held here on the first Sunday in June. Keep an eye on the calendar for the Women's Weekend every summer, along with Lazy Bear Weekend in early August, and Polar Bear Weekend in mid-January.

Address 16220 Main Street, Guerneville, CA 95446, +1 (707) 869-0206, www.queersteer.com | Getting there By car, from US-101, take exit 494 onto River Road and continue 15 miles to Main Street in Guerneville. | Hours Sun–Thu 2pm–midnight, Fri & Sat 2pm–2am | Tip At King's Sporting Goods & Kayak Rentals, you can pick up all the fishing supplies you need, from bait to fly rods and lines (16258 Main Street, Guerneville, www.kingsrussianriver.wixsite.com/kingsrussianriver).

85 Rancho de Petaluma
Back to the 1830s

East of Petaluma, along Old Adobe Road, you'll come across a state historic park devoted to the largest privately-owned adobe building in Northern California, built in 1836. It once belonged to Mariano Vallejo and his wife. He was that remarkable 19th-century figure, a military officer and rancher, who owned a good deal of property in Sonoma. He was also a founding father of California. He once noted that when he first saw this part of the county he was smitten.

The rancho was not so much a summer home – Vallejo had a few of those – as much as it was the headquarters of a vast ranch, where Vallejo managed his hide and tallow business, raised cattle, horses and sheep, and grew various crops. Every October, the ranch came to life during the Matanzas, when *hacendados* and field workers from the area gathered to slaughter pigs and cows, and, in recognition of the uncertainty of farm and ranch life, cooked every part of the animals. Afterwards, they enjoyed different kinds of folk dancing. The *fandango*, a dance celebration featuring violins and harps, was for the workers. The *baile* was another, more formal style of dancing for the owners and managers. The Vallejos often attended.

One secret of the rancho's early viability was a seven-mile creek that brought water for drinking and irrigation. However, eventually it became polluted and all but dried up. Restoration began in the early 1980s, and today, even with the drought, it survives. As you walk through the park, you may see red-shouldered hawks, barn owls, and possibly coyotes and foxes. Look for the native oaks and those most lush, white-flowered California buckeyes. As for the rancho itself, it's a two-story adobe structure with verandas. The adobe bricks are a blend of sand, clay, water, and straw. The house contains authentic furniture and, if you listen carefully, you can almost hear violins and harps.

Address 3325 Old Adobe Road, Petaluma, CA 94954, +1 (707) 762-4871, www.parks.ca.gov | Getting there By car, from US-101, take exit 472B onto Lakeville Street toward Sonoma, then turn left onto Frates Road, and left onto Old Adobe Road. | Hours Daily 10am−5pm | Tip Go for a paddle on the Petaluma River by renting a board or getting a lesson at Petaluma Stand Up Paddle (1075 Lakeville Street, Petaluma, www.napavalleypaddle.com/petaluma).

86 Rancho Obi-Wan
Where the Force is stored

It's as if you've opened an unmarked closet door and discovered the secret control room of the cultural/industrial complex known as *Star Wars*. Welcome to a museum presenting memorabilia from every last corner of that fictional universe.

The Rancho Obi-Wan museum, once a barn on a chicken ranch, is located west of Petaluma, down a country road, in a gated community, and in someone's private home. You must purchase a thankfully affordable membership to get the address. No secrets are revealed here.

The museum, a nonprofit organization, holds the world's largest Star Wars memorabilia collection, which was certified by Guinness World Records in 2014. The collection includes more than 500,000 items, of which one percent are on display at any one time. The museum, which is international in scope, is filled with memorabilia, including toys, games, "immersive environments," fan-made items, costumes, figurines, and props, some very rare. Don't miss the holographic chess game creatures, which strangely have never been mass marketed and sold. There are various iterations of lightsabers; versions of stormtrooper helmets, including a steam punk version; a Japanese-made Samurai Vader; and R2D2 on skis. There's also *a Star Wars* Arcade, featuring vintage video games and pinball machines, all set to free-play.

Tours last two to four hours and are designed for both casual and obsessive fans. Docents are serious students of *Star Wars* culture. One is a member of the Golden Gate Garrison, a Bay Area chapter of the 501st Legion, an international *Star Wars* costuming club focused on Imperial-style regalia. The person who so lovingly put this all together and keeps it together is Steve Sansweet, the former director of content management and head of fan relations at Lucasfilm LTD. He's a congenial character, who sometimes leads tours himself and is dedicated to inspiring people.

Address Petaluma, CA. You must become a member of Rancho Obi-Wan to learn the museum's address. | **Getting there** You'll receive directions when you book your tour. | **Hours** Tours Sat 10am by reservation | **Tip** Stop at Petaluma Collective Antiques, and you just may find some *Star Wars* memorabilia for your own collection (300 Petaluma Boulevard N, Petaluma, www.sonoma.com/businesses/42681/petaluma-collective).

87 Reared In Steel
Burning Man sculptures

First held in 1986 on Baker Beach in San Francisco, Burning Man now takes place each year in Black Rock City, Nevada. Recent organizers define Burning Man as "a city wherein almost everything that happens is created by its citizens, who are active participants in the experience." It's a setting for an experiment in artistic expression, fast-tracked community development, fantastic attire, and self-reliance in a harsh desert environment.

At the end of each year's burning, the creative structures are trucked back to garages, warehouses, and metal art studios. You'll find one such studio just west of Highway 101 in Petaluma. It's called Reared In Steel, inspired by Hank Rearden, the self-made steel magnate in Ayn Rand's *Atlas Shrugged*.

The studio's principal artist is Kevin Clark, whose Burning Man sculptures include the enormous *Medusa Madness*; 70-foot-tall *Flower Tower*; and a mech-lion *Guardino Leone*; The *Mad Max*-like motorized rhinoceros called *Rhino Redemption* has a body built on a 1974 Chevy pickup frame. Each side is fitted with curtains that can be opened to reveal a small musical stage. Fire can shoot out the rhino's horn. Clark is also considering creating a public display on the studio's perimeter fence to answer typical questions from people stopping to take a closer look.

You can see more Burning Man sculptures in Sonoma County at the large, outdoor sculpture garden at Paradise Ridge Winery. The impressive *Empyrean Temple* is displayed on the winery's hillside, waiting to be an official temple at the next Burning Man. It was built in Santa Rosa by Laurence Renzo Verbeck and Sylvia Adrienne Lisse. At Soda Rock in Healdsburg, you'll find a 20-foot-tall, 30-foot-long boar sculpture *Lord Snort*, an enormous, rotating, metal boar. And at Wilson Winery is the 26-foot-tall *The Coyote*. Both sculptures were made by Bryan Tedrick.

Address 110 Copeland Street, Petaluma, CA 94952, www.facebook.com/rearedinsteel |
Getting there By car, from US-101, take exit 474 onto E Washington Street toward
central Petaluma and turn right onto Copeland Street. | Hours Unrestricted from the
outside only | Tip Cinnabar Theater hosts a variety of professional shows, including
musicals, drama, comedy, a cabaret show and opera (3333 Petaluma Boulevard N,
Petaluma, www.cinnabartheater.org).

88__Rio Nido Lodge
Russian River gem

Ada Limón, the 2022 Poet Laureate of the United States, grew up in Sonoma County and once wrote a poem entitled *The Russian River*. She wrote, "It was the summer of our final year of high school, we were all so stoned that the world was perfectly defined by goodness and realness and the opposite of those…. Outside of Guerneville we found the party – beautiful bodies jumping off the cliffs, a raft of natural naked women floating like an old cigarette ad down the current. I was going to marry you…."

Such was the carefree splendor and earnest promise of the Russian River in the early 1990s, somehow also resembling the spirit of the 1930s at Rio Nido.

In Rio Nido, you'll find the historic Rio Nido Lodge, a few minutes' drive east of Guerneville. The lodge, just across the street from the river, was the playground for San Francisco's elite in the 1930s and became one of the most popular spots on the river. The dining room served Italian food, and in the lounge, heavy-handed martinis were served. Guests included Big Band musicians, such as Harry James, Woody Herman, and Ozzie Nelson. The musicians played at a dance hall down the street but hung out at the lodge. You never knew who might sit down at the piano or next to you.

The Rio Nido lodge was built in 1915 in a Tudor style. There are 11 guest rooms, mixing rustic and modern touches, along with hot tubs. The lodge has a large banquet hall, a lounge and a billiards game room, leather chesterfield sofas, vintage crystal cut glasses, and floor-to-ceiling river rock fireplaces. Outside, there are several fire pits, a bocce ball court, and a horseshoe pit. There are two detached cottages with full kitchens. Stop in at a morning time coffee shop that serves locally roasted coffee and local pastries. The lodge hosts guest events, such as murder mystery dinners, champagne & burlesque shows, paint & sip nights, tea parties, and an 80s prom party.

Address 4444 Wood Road, Guerneville, CA 95446, +1 (707) 604-8565, www.rionidolodge.com, rionidolodge2.0@gmail.com | Getting there By car, from US-101, take exit 494 onto River Road, continue 14 miles, then turn right onto Canyon Two Road, and left onto Wood Road. | Hours Call for reservations | Tip Enjoy a swim at Rio Nido Roadhouse Pool, which has a lifeguard on duty so the whole family can play. It's open weekends from Memorial Day through Labor Day (14540 Canyon Two Road, www.rionidoroadhouse.com/pool).

89 Robert Ferguson Observatory

Hiking to Pluto

The Robert Ferguson Observatory in Sugarloaf Ridge State Park opened in several stages between 1997 and 2003. It's named after amateur astronomer Robert Ferguson, who sought to develop a fully functioning observatory as a community resource. In fact, much of the construction was done with the help of volunteers. Ferguson also strongly encouraged the study of astronomy in local schools, and each year he rewarded serious students with free telescopes that he made himself.

Robert Ferguson Observatory operates the three basic types of telescope designs: refracting, reflecting, and catadioptric. The reflector telescope here is the largest in Northern California that is accessible to the public. It features a 40-inch-diameter parabolic mirror that weighs a third of a ton and has a focal length of 3,600 mm. Attached to the main telescope is an eight-inch spotting scope, along with a Telrad finder for "star hopping."

What makes the Ferguson Observatory unusual, particularly for the casual visitor to the heavens, is *PlanetWalk*, a scale model of the solar system laid out within the boundaries of Sugarloaf Park. In effect, the solar system has been reduced 2,360,000,000 times, enabling you to grasp vast distances in the universe as you go on a four-and-a-half mile round-trip hike. The trail winds along a ridge and past nine trail signs, all the way to the orbit of the dwarf planet Pluto. Each planet sign is set at the proportional distance from the *PlanetWalk* Sun, located near the main building. The trail was destroyed in the 2017 fires but has since been restored. Star Parties are held throughout the year. At the observatory's visitor center, you'll be able to find binoculars, guides, warmers, red flashlights, safe solar glasses, and planispheres.

Address 2605 Adobe Canyon Road, Kenwood, CA 95452, +1 (707) 833-6979, www.rfo.org, info@rfo.org | Getting there By car, from US-101, take exit 488A onto CA-12 toward Sonoma, continue for eight miles, and turn left onto Adobe Canyon Road. Or take CA-12 north from Sonoma and turn right onto Adobe Canyon Road. | Hours Park: daily dawn–dusk; Observatory: see website for event schedule | Tip Stop at Swede's Feeds Pet and Garden for a collection of hand-made folk art pieces made from recycled oil barrels and machinery gears. You can also buy pet food and supplies, plants, and garden materials (9140 Sonoma Highway, Kenwood, www.swedesfeeds.com).

90 Robert Ripley's Grave
Odd man out

Robert Ripley, the merchant of strange, was born in Santa Rosa on Christmas Day, 1893. He died in New York City in 1949 and was buried in his hometown in the old part of the Odd Fellows Lot Cemetery on Franklin Avenue, part of Santa Rosa Memorial Park. And yes, what an odd coincidence that the aficionado of odd, and a man who made the public fascination with the bizarre into a big business, should be resting in peace in an Odd Fellows Cemetery. The Odd Fellows is a fraternal order of craftsmen that sprang up in the mid 1700s in England and pledged themselves to good deeds, especially to "visit the sick, relieve the distressed, bury the dead and educate the orphan."

Ripley was an amateur anthropologist, an author and radio broadcaster, and a talented cartoonist. He then transitioned his program into the first "reality TV" show. He was also a sports fanatic who set out to become a professional baseball pitcher. But in his first appearance in the minors, he broke his pitching arm and so turned to drawing cartoons. He soon stumbled on to a new perspective: he drew a cartoon with a series of panels each with an unusual fact from baseball. Gradually, he expanded this format to all kinds of unusual facts.

Ripley became wildly popular and wealthy in the 1930s and 40s. He traveled the world looking for weird rituals, unexpected science facts, and even people otherwise labeled "circus freaks," all of which he displayed in what he called "Odditoriums." (These days, the Ripley organization is careful to say that to Ripley [freaks] were the ultimate underdogs, wonders of nature and worthy of happy lives.")

Ripley himself lived a life of "believe it or not." He never learned to drive but was an avid car collector. He collected boats but didn't swim. In May 1949, while on stage discussing *Taps*, the military funeral anthem, he suffered a heart attack and died.

Address 1900 Franklin Avenue, Santa Rosa, CA 95404, +1 (707) 542-1580 | Getting there By car, from US-101, take exit 490 onto Steele Lane, continue onto Lewis Road, and turn left onto Franklin Avenue. | Hours Mon–Sat 8am–4:30pm | Tip Visit the Environmental Discovery Center or cool off in the seasonal swimming lagoon at nearby Spring Lake Regional Park (5585 Newanga Avenue, Santa Rosa, parks.sonomacounty.ca.gov/visit/find-a-park/spring-lake-regional-park).

91 __ Sea Ranch

Living lightly on the land

The original 1963 Sea Ranch sales brochure read, "The terrain is rugged, the surf treacherous, the ocean cold." Believe it or not, this description was meant to paint a positive picture of this coastal community.

Sea Ranch was founded in 1960 and was based on environmental tenets: common land use, shared ocean views, and blending buildings with nature rather than individual expression. The concept was inspired by The New Towns Movement, which took root in Britain after World War II. It followed the Garden City Movement and was imagined as an antidote to "urban disease." Alfred Boeke (1922–2011), a developer deeply motivated by the New Towns Movement, fell in love with a 10-mile stretch of Sonoma coastline and enlisted several top architects – and one top landscape architect, Lawrence Halprin – to create 2,000 houses on 5,200 acres of unincorporated land that was once a sheep ranch.

One of the architects Boeke chose was Charles Willard Moore (1925–1993), sometimes referred to as the "father of postmodernism." His signature at Sea Ranch was timber-frame, vertically-oriented structures, with slanted roofs reminiscent of mining sheds. Vincent Scully, the preeminent architectural historian, once noted, "Sea Ranch influenced the revival of American vernacular architecture in wood, as part of the reaction against the International style in the 1960s. Moore's buildings there are in the spirit of California – laid-back shack architecture from which even the work of Frank Gehry derived."

You can experience these idealistic housing communities set in the rugged and beautiful environment just by spending time walking around on the path or climbing down to one of the many white sandy beaches. There are six public access points to the coast and miles of hiking trails. You can also catch the sunset at Sea Ranch Lodge where you can go for drinks and dinner.

Address Sea Ranch Lodge, 60 Sea Walk Drive, Sea Ranch, CA 95497, +1 (707) 579-9777, www.thesearanchlodge.com, info@thesearanchlodge.com | Getting there By car, from US-101, take exit 494 to River Road W, drive 27 miles, turn right onto CA-1, and then drive 30 miles to the destination. | Hours Daily dawn–dusk | Tip Located at the south end of Sea Ranch is Stewarts Point Store, offering delicious breakfasts and lunches and homemade bread (32000 Highway 1, Stewarts Point, www.twofishbaking.co).

92 Sea Ranch Chapel

A spiritual place where art meets nature

Among the unusual structures at Sea Ranch is a 360-square-foot, non-denominational chapel five miles north of the Sea Ranch Lodge on Highway 1. It rests in a meadow surrounded by redwoods, oaks, and evergreen shrubs.

The chapel was designed in 1984 by James Hubbell and built by local artisans. It's a perfect example of Hubbell's philosophy around creating organic and unique living environments for humans to dwell in harmony with nature. It has a bird-like quality, as though a creature is about to take off. From another angle, the chapel suggests the helmet of a *conquistador*, a shell, or a cresting wave, but its nickname is the "Mushroom Church" for reasons that are obvious when you see it.

Hubbell's inspiration for the chapel was the whimsical drawings of a one-time Navy pilot and artist named Kirk Ditzler. Hubbell created a ceramic model that became the blueprint. The roof's windswept pattern is made from cedar shingles on a frame fashioned by a boat builder. The interior combines plaster ceilings and locally harvested redwood siding. Everything in the space is a work of art and made with materials found nearby whenever possible. Take your time to look at the carved benches, the tall and colorful stained-glass windows, a sculpted metal chandelier, and the seashells set in the ceiling. The floor is natural stone inlaid with a floral mosaic.

The chapel conveys the original spirit of Sea Ranch, a place planned around nature, not the other way around. Or rather, the chapel's uniqueness is juxtaposing the rest of the Sea Ranch buildings, whose characteristics are the simple exteriors controlled by rigid guidelines. Every detail here is managed, from the stained wood siding to the native plants in front of the building.

The chapel is a place for prayer and meditation, reading a book, simply getting away, or maybe even contemplating whale journeys.

Address 40033 Highway 1, Sea Ranch, CA 95497, +1 (707) 785-2444, www.thesearanchchapel.org | Getting there By car, from US-101, take exit 494 to River Road W and continue for 27 miles. Turn right onto CA-1, and then drive 35 miles to the destination. | Hours Daily dawn–dusk | Tip Stop at Gualala Art Center, a community arts organization with numerous outdoor art installations, a gallery, and a theater (46501 Old Stage Road, Gualala, www.gualalaarts.org).

93__Sebastiani Movie Theater
A cinema's verité

The Sebastiani Movie Theater opened on the Sonoma Plaza, the town commons, in 1934 during a decade in which the Great Depression intersected with the Golden Age of Hollywood. The theater's first showing was *Fugitive Lovers*, a comedy / crime film starring B-movie actors and the Three Stooges. For nearly 20 years, the theater flourished, hosting at least one local premier, the 1941 version of *The Sea Wolf*, starring Edward G. Robinson and based on the Jack London novel. London lived in nearby Glen Ellen until his death in 1916.

In the 1950s, Hollywood's great age collapsed under the weight of television. Small-town theaters began to struggle. Beginning in the 1960s, the Sebastiani Theatre went through a series of owners, most of whom were unable to sustain the relentless upkeep of the theater itself. Fortunately, in recent years, the theater's Sebastiani Foundation has righted things. The theater occasionally plays first-run features, as well as film classics and documentaries, and hosts festivals, local musicians, and theatrical performances, including the likes of the San Francisco Mime Troupe. Local premiers have included Francis Coppola's *Tucker* (1988) and Sonoma's own John Lasseter's *Toy Story* (1995).

The theater was the dreamchild of the vine baron Samuele Sebastiani, who hired the great movie house architect James W. Reid and his brother Merritt. They were known for Italian Renaissance designs and the use of steel. Notable Reid buildings in San Francisco include the Fairmont Hotel and the Cliff House Restaurant, along with a string of movie theaters in the Bay Area.

The interior railings and doors are made of oak barrel staves from a Sacramento brewery, with mosaic tiles on the foyer floor. You'll find a ballroom on the second floor. In front of the theater, a mannequin known as Trixie mans the original ticket booth that still stands under the marquee.

Address 476 1st Street E, Sonoma, CA 95476, +1 (707) 996-9756, www.sebastianitheaterfoundation.org, info@sebastianitheatrefoundation.org | **Getting there** By car, take CA-12/Broadway to Sonoma Plaza, turn right onto E Napa Street, and left onto 1st Street E. | **Hours** See website for schedule | **Tip** Each Tuesday evening from May through September, you can enjoy fresh produce from local farmers and live music at Sonoma Tuesday Night Market (The Plaza, Sonoma, www.sonomastuesdaynightmarket.com).

94 Skippy's Egg Store
Once the egg basket of the world

In 1918, a "booster extraordinaire" named Bert Kerrigan proclaimed Petaluma the "Egg Basket of the World." Kerrigan dreamed up National Egg Day, which actually lasted several days. The celebrations included a parade with floats and costumes, an Egg Queen, the Egg Ball, and an Egg Day Rodeo of hens and horses. There was a "chicken chase" shadowed by a biplane up in the sky dropping chicken feathers stuck to coupons that you could redeem for eggs from Petaluma.

The local invention of the Bryce-Dias coal lamp egg incubator in 1879 by a medical student Lyman Bryce and a Petaluma dentist Isaac Dias led to more hatcheries to meet the increasing demand for eggs.

The poultry business took off, and by 1915, Petaluma, which had its own seaport, was regarded as one of the richest little cities in the Americas. Eggs became a theme – there was even a chicken pharmacy that specialized in remedies for sick chickens. In the 1940s, the Petaluma poultry empire peaked with 36 commercial hatcheries. In 1945, Sonoma County produced 51 million dozen eggs. Then decline. In the 1950's small farms were bought up. Some of the old chicken sheds are still standing, often with their roofs caved in and paint peeled off.

In the 1980s, the parade was resurrected. The "Butter and Egg Days Parade & Festival" is organized and hosted by Petaluma Egg Farm. Steve and Judy Mahrt started the farm in 1983, but the family history of raising the chickens for eggs started back in the early 1900s, with a hatchery in Calistoga. You can purchase their wide variety of farm-fresh eggs at Skippy's Eggs Store, which is both a store and an egg history museum, located in East Petaluma, at the back of a yellow and blue warehouse building. The Mahrts have been collecting everything egg-related for many years. The museum presents how the egg business has progressed over the time.

Address 951 Transport Way, Petaluma, CA 94954, +1 (707) 763-2924, www.skippyseggstore.com | Getting there By car, from US-101, take exit 474 onto E Washington Street east, then turn left onto N McDowell Boulevard and left onto Transport Way. | Hours Mon–Fri 8am–4:30pm, Sat 8am–noon | Tip For a delicious eggs benedict, stop at Sax's Joint (317 Petaluma Boulevard S, Petaluma).

95 Sonoma Botanical Garden
Where California meets East Asia

The Sonoma Botanical Garden, located in the foothills of the Maya-camas Mountains, is formally known as Quarryhill. It contains one of the largest collections of "scientifically documented" Asian plants in North America and Europe. By one estimate, there are 25,000 plants, started from wild-collected seeds.

Jane Davenport Jensen (1940–2000) began the Sonoma Botanical Garden in 1987. She had purchased the abandoned sandstone quarry site a year before to start the center for the cultivation of rare seeds and endangered plants she had gathered and brought back from annual scientific trips to China. She first established a small nursery to cultivate the seeds and then began planting them in 1990. The 61 acres of land host a 25-acre Asian woodland garden, 22 acres of California native oak savanna, and a small plot of Cabernet vines.

The wild Asian woodland garden is lush, with towering trees and shrubs on the hilly terrain. It includes primarily plants from temperate climes in Japan, China, Taiwan, India, and the Himalayas, including Tibet and Nepal. Keep your eye out to spot rare Asian dogwoods, magnolias, oaks, and maples, along with lilies and rhododendrons. You'll find the rarest and most endangered maple in the world, *Acer pentaphyllum*. All plants are marked with identification numbers and information about the species and source.

The gardens stay open all year. Be sure to wear sturdy shoes, as you'll begin by walking up a steep hill and continue along trail paths that are narrow, winding, and well kept. Take a deep breath to smell the burnt brown-sugar scent of the katsura trees. The pond and the waterfalls are perfect places to relax and to view this artful woodland landscape. This garden will transport you to the native habitats in Asia, with new and delightful colors, textures, and scents every season, so visit during different times of the year.

Address 12841 Sonoma Highway, Glen Ellen, CA 95442, +1 (707) 996-3166, www.sonomabg.org, info@sonomabg.org | **Getting there** By car, take CA-12 about seven miles north of Sonoma to the destination. | **Hours** Wed–Mon 9am–4pm | **Tip** Stop by at Imagery Estate Winery & Art Gallery to enjoy a fine glass of wine and some of the winery's art from its collection of 600 works (14335 Sonoma Highway, Glen Ellen, www.imagerywinery.com).

96 Sonoma County Wildlife Rescue

A residential facility for banged up wild animals

The eight-acre Sonoma County Wildlife Rescue is a nonprofit organization founded in 1981 by a small group of women dedicated to wildlife rehabilitation and public education.

Today, a skilled team cares for the rescued animals. Patients include the raccoon baby who got his head stuck in a hole, the gray fox with his leg caught in a fence, the skunk stuck in a drainpipe, and the bear cubs injured in local fires. Or the mountain lion with a neurological disorder. Care includes surgery and often a lengthy process of healing and rehabilitation. Eighty percent of patients are released back into the wild. They'll help almost 1500 animals in need of care per year. As they posted on their Facebook page, most of the admissions are caused by human conflict on wildlife habitats.

Rescue extends mostly to mammals and raptors, particularly hawks, owls, and eagles, as well as doves and crows – but not to turkeys, songbirds, deer, or rodents. The center provides tours and field trips, which are perfect for anyone who's interested in the art and science of wildlife rehabilitation. They also offer educational seminars, like "How to coexist with Wild Cats in the Bay Area."

The center performs educational outreach programs and hosts an educational barnyard, where you can learn techniques to separate domestic and wild animals. You'll see a space for free range chickens, and a "catio" - a patio enclosure for cats. There's also a night corral to keep livestock safe in the dark. In recent years, the center has developed Apex pens to protect livestock from mountain lions and bears. For a fee, rescue staff will come to your home or farm and help develop "exclusion" strategies. They can also install and maintain a barn owl box to entice owls to settle in your barn and perform pest control.

Address 403 Mecham Road, Petaluma, CA 94952, +1 (707) 992-0274, www.scwildliferescue.org, education@scwildliferescue.org | **Getting there** By car, from US-101, take exit 479 onto W Railroad Avenue, then turn right onto Stony Point Road and left onto Mecham Road. | **Hours** Tours by appointment, May–Sep Sat noon & 2pm, Oct–April Sat 2pm | **Tip** Enjoy some solitude during quieter times of the day at Crane Creek Park (5000 Pressley Road, Rohnert Park, parks.sonomacounty.ca.gov).

97 __ Sonoma Mountain Zen Center

A clear path to community

Among the Buddhist retreat centers north of San Francisco, many of the most notable ones can be found in Sonoma County and Marin. The biggest and one of the most beautiful retreat centers is Odiyan, sometimes referred to as the Copper Mountain Temple. It's located in Cazadero, not far from Sea Ranch. But this retreat is private and only open to those interested in six-month apprenticeships.

Luckily, a much smaller and very humble Buddhist retreat called the Sonoma Mountain Zen Center welcomes the public. It lies northwest of Glen Ellen on Sonoma Mountain Road, among California oak and manzanita groves above the Valley of the Moon. This retreat is a classical Soto Zen practice center founded by Jakusho Kwong-roshi and his wife Laura Shinko Kwong in 1973.

It's a pristine and heavenly place, where you'll find a Japanese temple with a hint of California barn style. The temple is dedicated to Zazen, an act of "just sitting." Kodo Sawaki Rōshi, the great Zen master of early 20th-century Japan, said, "Just sit *zazen*, and that's the end of it." Soto Zen Buddhism is distinguished by its focus on the down-to-earth practice of "everyday Zen," a meditation focused on letting go of earthly thoughts. It encourages awareness of the workings of one's own mind as a means of living mindfully in all areas of daily life.

The Sonoma Mountain Zen Center welcomes drop-ins during morning and evening *zazen* periods in the zendo, and visitors are also invited to join in daily temple life. You're encouraged to enjoy this solitude by doing some reading or writing, or even going for a hike. The Temple Stay meditation program starts at 3pm on Friday. Bedtime is at 8:55pm, and everyone wakes up at 5am the next morning for more meditation and lunch before checking out at 1pm. Families with children are welcome to participate in the Saturday Community Program.

Address 6367 Sonoma Mountain Road, Santa Rosa, CA 95404, +1 (707) 545-8105, www.smzc.org, office@smzc.org | Getting there By car, from US-101, take exit 483 onto Rohnert Park Expressway and turn right onto Petaluma Hill. Turn left onto Robert Road, continue onto Pressley Road, and turn right onto Sonoma Mountain Road. | **Hours** Daily 9:15am – 3:30pm | Tip Located on the same road are the organically farmed Van der Kamp vineyards, one of the oldest producers of pinot noir (6360 Sonoma Mountain Road, Santa Rosa, www.vanderkampvineyard.com).

98 Sonoma Raceway

Screeching tires, white smoke; drag and drift

Sonoma Raceway was originally called Sears Point, named after a local 19th-century landowner. The racetrack itself is set in the Sonoma Mountains. It opened in 1968 and favored motorcycle events through the 1970s. The venue, which is much larger than it appears as you drive past, has 47,000 permanent seats, but it can accommodate up to 102,000 fans for special races. The hilly, full-length road course has 12 turns and is just over 2.5 miles long.

The raceway includes a 440-yard dragstrip and hosts more than a dozen series, including a NASCAR Cup, 24 Hours of Le Mans, the Ferrari Challenge, The National Hot Rod Association, and the American Federation of Motorcyclists (AFM).

On Wednesday nights from April to August, the raceway opens up to amateur racing designed for teenagers and supervised by local law enforcement. Any teenager with a high school ID, a driver's license, and 15 dollars for registration can come to Sonoma Raceway to race against a uniformed police officer in a squad car down the quarter-mile strip. It's a popular event. Between races, the officers offer tips to teenagers on safe driving.

Wednesday Night Drags involve drag racing on the quarter-mile track. The original idea was to get dragsters to race their cars here and not on city streets, for obvious public safety reasons. The races are started electronically by a system known as a Christmas tree, which consists of a column of seven lights for each driver or lane, as well as a set of light beams across the track.

Running alongside the drags is Sonoma Drift. This is where drivers practice "drifting," which involves sliding at speed on a specially prepared surface in the paddock area. The goal is not time but to demonstrate "style and execution." If you'd like to try it, almost any car will do. They give your car a technical check, and off you go. The drag racing is also open to any licensed driver.

Address 29355 Arnold Drive, Sonoma, CA 95476, +1 (800) 870-7223, www.sonomaraceway.com | Getting there By car, from US-101, take exit 460A onto CA-37 E and then turn left onto Arnold Drive. | Hours See website for event schedule | Tip Close by is the Ram's Gate Winery, a perfect stop to enjoy wine and food pairings on the veranda with an open fire (28700 Carneros Highway, Sonoma, www.ramsgatewinery.com).

99 __ Sonoma Valley Airport

Wine Country from the air

You can tour the wine country by balloon, bike, bus, glider, limo, or train – or from vintage airplanes that fly out of Sonoma Valley Airport. Locals call it Schellville Airport, a two-strip aviator heaven about four miles south of Sonoma Plaza. Built in 1946, this airport now serves the small-plane aficionados, who call it the "home of the taildraggers."

The airport has two tenants. The North Bay Air Museum focuses on World War II fighters, including a North American P-51 Mustang, about which Luftwaffe commander Hermann Göring reportedly said, "When I saw Mustangs over Berlin, I knew the jig was up." The museum also features the Massachusetts Air National Guard F-15 Eagle, which was the first fully armed plane that responded to the 9/11 terrorist attack in New York City. Look for the Curtiss P-40 Kittyhawk, best known for use by The Flying Tigers early in the war. Amazingly, you can even ride in these planes for a fee. It's not inexpensive by most standards, but you'll zip along at more than 350 mph.

The Vintage Aircraft Company, the second tenant here, offers rides in open-cockpit biplanes, a less expensive option more for sightseeing than thrill-seeking. There are several planes to choose from, including three Boeing PT-17 Stearman, which were built as basic trainers in 1942. You have a choice of flight plans. One covers the wine country east from the airport to Napa, then north to Saint Helena and west to Glen Ellen. Another plan runs southwest over Novato and west to Tomales Bay. A third route flies you south to the Golden Gate Bridge, around Mt. Tamalpais, and up to Point Reyes.

You can also experience some aerobatics firsthand, say a barrel roll and a hammerhead. You'll be strapped into a biplane with a parachute, and you'll be sitting next to your companion in the front seat on a 32-inch-wide bench. It's close quarters – and thrilling.

Address 23982 Arnold Drive, Sonoma, CA 95476; North Bay Air Museum: +1 (707) 934-5158, www.northbayairmuseum.org, northbayairmuseum@gmail.com; Vintage Aircraft Company: +1 (707) 938-2444, www.vintageaircraft.com | Getting there By car, from US-101, take exit 460A onto CA-37 E, and then turn left onto Arnold Drive. | Hours See websites for hours, events, and reservations | Tip Viansa Winery, with beautiful views of the valley, is just a mile south of the airport (25200 Arnold Drive, Sonoma, www.viansa.com).

100 Sonoma Zipline Adventures

Flying through the treetops at 40 mph

In 1946, several pastors joined together to buy 76 acres off the Bohemian Highway in what is now Occidental, California, about 20 minutes from the ocean. They imagined a place where they could bring families and children to experience the wondrous redwood forests. The plan worked, and the nonprofit Alliance Redwoods Conference Grounds is particularly well known today for its children's science camp with a foundation in Christian spirituality. It is also a conference center that serves thousands of visitors every year. In 2008, the Alliance came upon the idea of ziplining. During the 1970s, wildlife biologists in Costa Rica built so-called "zip-lines," rope and pulley systems leveraging gravity, to study natural habitats without disturbing them.

Your extraordinary treetop adventure begins with a climb up suspended staircases spiraling up redwood trees to the canopy. The views are spectacular! Suddenly you're in a world of sky bridges, ziplines, and yurts where you can spend the night. There are two main zipline courses with a total of 14 segments covering more than a mile. The original course takes two and a half hours, using seven zip lines strung up to 250 feet above the ground at the highest point. You're traveling at 30 mph – faster if you can streamline your body. And on the newer course, you can reach 40 mph. Two guides accompany you, one on the tree you're approaching, and one on the tree you've just left. The guides control the brakes. At the end of your journey, you'll rappel 60 feet down to the ground. You'll probably wish you could keep on flying.

Children must weigh at least 70 pounds and be at least 10 years old, and adults cannot weigh more than 250 pounds. Sleeping four to five people, each yurt is compliant with building regulations. If you choose to stay overnight, plans include a gourmet dinner, breakfast, and a zipline adventure.

Address 6250 Bohemian Highway, Occidental, CA 95465, +1 (888) 494-7868, www.sonomacanopytours.com, info@sonomacanopytours.com | Getting there By car, from US-101, take exit 488B onto CA-12 W towards Sebastopol. Turn right onto Fulton Road, left onto Occidental Road, right onto Green Hill Road, left onto Graton Road, and right onto Bohemian Highway. | Hours By appointment only | Tip Reserve a time to see the ponds, bridges, and large variety of plants at Western Hills Garden (16250 Coleman Valley Road, Occidental, www.westernhillsgarden.com).

101 _Spoonfall_
Confluence, to the genius of Ned Kahn

Artist Ned Kahn is an engineer and conceptualist, a philosopher of space, weather, and technology, long fascinated by the "confluence of science and art." His genius is working with wind, water, fire, fog, sand, and, of course, light.

"I have developed a body of work inspired by atmospheric physics, geology, astronomy and fluid motion," he has written. "I strive to create artworks that enable viewers to observe and interact with natural processes. I am less interested in creating an alternative reality than I am in capturing the mysteriousness of the world around us." His work appears all over the world but primarily on the West Coast.

When you're in Healdsburg, go look for his work entitled _Spoonfall_ in the entryway of the stylish H2 Hotel and Spoonbar restaurant. Completed in 2010, H2 Hotel is the product of David Becker Architects, Marie Fisher Interior Design, and landscape architect Andrea Cochran. Using 2,000 espresso spoons designed to fill and spill, the artwork is a futuristic mill. Khan integrated the piece into the hotel's rain collection system, and it creates the sound of raindrops falling. One of the most interesting aspects of Kahn's works is how they often appear as partitions or borders, as does _Spoonfall_. In that sense, they become comments on the permeability of separation.

Look for Kahn's _Erratic Fence_ on the roof of the Santa Rosa Sonoma County Museum. Kahn's website describes _Microturbines_ at the Santa Rosa Junior College Student Center as "an array of 1,008 small, extruded acrylic turbines that spin in the wind." The side of the AT&T building in Santa Rosa is covered with a field of 30,000 wind-animated panels in a work called _Digitized Field_. And look for _Wind House_ at the di Rosa Art and Nature Preserve in Napa. Khan has had exhibitions at The Center for the Arts in Sebastopol, which is where his studios are located.

Address 219 Healdsburg Avenue, Healdsburg, CA 95448, www.nedkahn.com/portfolio/
spoonfall | **Getting there** By car, from US-101, take exit 503 toward Central Healdsburg and
continue onto Healdsburg Avenue. | **Hours** Unrestricted | **Tip** Take your time to explore the
town's romantic and historic Healdsburg Plaza (Healdsburg Avenue & Matheson Street,
Healdsburg).

102 __ Sturgeon's Mill

A mill's second act

In the late 1860s, lumber-cutting technology was powered by oxen, horses, and mules. Pine and redwood trees, always the lumber of choice for barns and houses, were cut and dragged down off the hills and out of the forest. When one area was exhausted, the mill was taken down and moved to another area. Eventually, animals were replaced by the steam-powered donkey, a technology derived from the motors used to raise sails on ships. The motors were made of metal and shaped like the Tin Man in the Wizard of Oz. The operator was called the "donkeyman." The process involved dragging cut trees using a system of cables and a machine called a yarder.

The logging boom of 1877 enabled the North Coast Railroad to crawl up through the Russian River Basin and fetch ever larger amounts of wood ever more quickly, particularly after the quakes and fires of 1906. In 1913, Wade and Ester Sturgeon and two friends bought 2,000 acres of land in Occidental's Coleman Valley and opened their mill. A crew of 10 jacks cut 15,000 feet of lumber a day, and the good times rolled. In 1923, Sturgeon followed the forest and moved the mill to Green Hill Road in Sebastopol, where it is today.

Eventually, the technology advanced and, unable to keep up, the mill closed in 1964. Miraculously, it reopened as a "working museum" nearly 30 years later. It makes for a worthy visit today. The mill is an oddly haunting tribute to the rusting donkeymen, the hand-tools they used, and their wagons and trucks. So many early 20th-century machines, once built to proud tolerances, now rest at the foot of the giant trees that might have once been cut. The steam-powered mill still fires up, and it's open to the public on certain summer weekends. More than 60 local volunteers have repaired and restored all the various pieces of equipment and now demonstrate the way the machines were operated.

Address 2150 Green Hill Road, Sebastopol, CA 95472, +1 (707) 829-2479, www.sturgeonsmill.com, info@sturgeonsmill.com | Getting there By car, from US-101, take exit 488B onto CA-12 W towards Sebastopol. Turn right onto Fulton Road, left onto Occidental Road, and right onto Green Hill Road. | Hours Unrestricted from the outside; see website for demonstration schedule | Tip A beautiful place to walk is the Grove of Old Trees, a 48-acre old growth stand of Coast Redwood trees (17599 Fitzpatrick Lane, Occidental, www.landpaths.org/grove-of-old-trees).

103 Tolay Lake

The power of charmstones

Tolay Lake was once a vast freshwater lake, full of perch and bass, and also a particularly sacred site for Coast Miwok and Southern Pomo Indians. Some archeologists consider it one of the three most significant gathering places for healing ceremonies among native Californians. Then a German immigrant farmer used dynamite to blow out a channel to drain the lake for grazing cattle and growing potatoes.

Today, the lakebed is a well-kept regional park. The land is largely flat, with herds of cows among few trees. There's a country road less traveled, most often by hikers and their dogs, and those who enjoy wide open spaces and the solitude to contemplate the lake's mysteries.

Once drained, Tolay Lake gave up its secrets. Among the shallows and mud were thousands of prehistoric objects, including arrowheads and so-called "charmstones." These charmstones, more than 4,000 years old, are oval-shaped and considered good luck by hunters and fishermen. They were made from a hard, gray stone called amphibolite schist, and they may also have been used as plummets or fishing weights. The most elaborately carved ones were found in graves. Some people believed the stones were alive and could be summoned to crawl up out of the mud.

Archeologists in the early 20th century interviewed Native Californians, including Ishi, who was likely the last member of the Yahi people, who described the ways in which these particular charmstones were used in ceremonies calling for rain. The stones were anointed with Datura, a plant that's both poisonous and hallucinogenic. Chairman of the Federated Indians of Graton Rancheria Greg Sarris, who is of Coast Miwok and Pomo descent, wrote in a 2017 *Bay Nature* article that the charmstones found in Lake Tolay are "the most significant discovery of cultural material for my people, but no doubt for all native people in California."

Address 5869 Cannon Lane, Petaluma, CA 94954, parks.sonomacounty.ca.gov | Getting there By car, from US-101, take exit 472B onto Lakeville Street toward Sonoma, then turn left onto Cannon Lane. | Hours Daily 7am–dusk | Tip No cellphones are allowed at Ernie's Tin Bar, a roadhouse 15 minutes north of Tolay. If you are caught on the phone, you have to buy a round for the bar (5100 Lakeville Highway, Petaluma).

104___ Train Town
A ride on the little kids' express

Disneyland, the original Disney amusement park in Anaheim, California opened in 1955 after a feasibility study was done by the Stanford Research Institute. What made the place an instant success was not only that you could meet Mickey Mouse and experience the nostalgia of Main Street, USA, but you could also enjoy the simple experience of having fun! Take, for example, the delightfully corny Jungle Cruise. At the end of your day, what you remembered was your jungle guide's engaging banter as much as the mechanical special effects. You took away a lifelong memory of a shared experience, rather than a passing adrenalin thrill.

And that's precisely the attraction of Train Town, an old fashioned, family-owned theme park that people have been coming to since it opened in 1968. It's a clean, well-maintained amusement park on 10 acres, with woods, ponds, waterfalls, and streams, all designed to entertain toddlers and kids up to age nine or so. The train motif is wildly popular among young aficionados. There's an actual steam train, built to one-quarter-size scale, that pulls six cars around a 15-gauge track. The town, built to the same scale, replicates the kind of place you'd find in the Sierra Nevada foothills during the Gold Rush in the 1850s.

The train ride lasts about 20 minutes, and there's a stop at a petting zoo with llamas and other animals. Other attractions include a carousel, a biplane ride, a Ferris wheel, a gentle rollercoaster, and a "locomotion scrambler" in which suspended riders spinning in cars experience centrifugal force. The park was created by Stanley Frank, who owned a printing business in Oakland and had a passion for trains. He built the engines and train cars himself, and he also constructed much of the scenery. The ambiance is friendly and easy, without the stress of long lines for short rides – just the opposite of a day at Disneyland.

Address 20264 Broadway, Sonoma, CA 95476, +1 (707) 938-3912, www.traintown.com |
Getting there By car, from CA-121/Arnold Road in Sonoma, turn onto Leveroni Road and
then turn left onto Broadway. | Hours See website for seasonal hours | Tip The duck pond
in Sonoma Plaza is a big hit with small kids, as is the playground on the plaza's west side
(453 1st Street E, Sonoma, www.sonomacity.org/the-plaza).

105 — Twin Oaks Tavern
For all kinds of cowboys since 1924

As you travel along the Old Redwood Highway between Petaluma and Cotati, you'll come to the town of Penngrove, California, with a population of 2,400 or so. Every year on the Sunday closest to the 4th of July, the Penngrove Social Firemen put on a patriotic parade. Penngrove has been a small-town kind of place since before the turn of the last century, when trains came here to transport cobblestones cut from local quarries for the streets of San Francisco, along with chickens and eggs. Today, the town remains out of the way – and out of the chicken business. It's now strictly a farming town in the exurbs, and its history remains an excerpt from Old Western times of Northern California. To see this intersection where the past meets the present, step inside the Twin Oaks Tavern.

Built in 1924, the tavern still looks much as it did back then, with exposed beams, a bar, a fireplace, a wooden dance floor that holds 40, and a beer garden in the back with live bands. It is one of four local taverns owned by the HopMonk Taverns, all known for hosting live, mostly eclectic Americana music. Groups like Johnny & June Forever, Miracle Mule, Heartwood Crossing, and Chuck Prophet & the Mission Express all perform here. There's also country line dancing every second and fourth Thursday.

Twin Oaks Tavern has long catered to its loyal customers, such as Johnny Debernardi, the self-proclaimed "Mayor of Penngrove" and a great storyteller - especially one particular story that he told a reporter from the *Argus Courier* in 2019. It's about the night at the tavern years ago when he died. The morbid event happened on his birthday no less, after too many shots of Jack Daniels. "I died in this place once, right here, for real. They called the coroner who pronounced me dead, put me in a body bag and everything. But I wasn't all the way dead, so here I am today. And that's the truth."

Address 5745 Old Redwood Highway N, Penngrove, CA 94951, +1 (707) 795-5118, www.hopmonk.com/twin-oaks | Getting there By car, from US-101, take exit 476 and turn right onto Old Redwood Highway N. | Hours Sun–Thu noon–9pm, Fri & Sat noon–11pm | Tip Visit the Penngrove Power and Implement Museum, a private collection of old tractors, vintage printing presses, and one of the engines from Howard Hughes' famous Spruce Goose H-4 Hercules (200 Phillips Drive, Penngrove, www.facebook.com/penngrovepower).

106 Union Hotel
Go back in time in Occidental

In the late 1870s, the North Pacific Coast Railroad opened a line from Sausalito to Cazadero. Folks from San Francisco caught a ferry to Sausalito, and off they went to find the redwoods. It was a narrow-gauge, mishap-prone line designed to carry timber, but gradually more and more tourists climbed aboard. Station stops included Tomales Bay, Bodega, Freestone, and Occidental.

A century and a half later, Occidental is a town of around 1,100. The population has been oddly wavering in recent years, but the place remains prosperous. These days, it's considered "alternative" too. The community was originally Italian, Catholic, closely knit, and politically conservative. But the Vietnam War led to a tale of two cities.

A counterculture arrived and flourished here in the 1960s and 70s, along with communes and a high society of textile makers, painters, potters, sculptors, ecologists, shamans, and musicians. The town's favorite residents include Grateful Dead drummer Mickey Hart and his wife Caryl, and Terrence McKenna (1946–2000), sometimes referred to as the "Timothy Leary of the 1990s," a truly charismatic figure and intellectual who believed in the positive influence of psilocybin mushrooms.

Another side of Occidental is represented by the Union Hotel, built in 1879 to house railroad crews. It's a place where tables are still covered in red-and-white-checkered tablecloths, where the scents of Italian cuisine - especially garlic - still permeate the dining room, and where locals still come to the hotel's Bocce ballroom at Christmas to sing carols. There's always live music coming from the saloon, and you will be warmly greeted by the fabulous smile of Barbara Gonnella, granddaughter of one of the town's great old families. The family still owns the hotel, the bakery, the saloon, and three luxury guest houses. As for the train, it stopped service in the 1930s.

Address 3731 Main Street, Occidental, CA 95465 , +1 (707) 874-3555,
www.unionhoteloccidental.com | Getting there By car, from US-101, take exit 488B onto
CA-12 W towards Sebastopol. Turn right onto Fulton Road, left onto Occidental Road,
right onto Green Hill Road, left onto Graton Road, and left onto Main Street. | Hours
Fri–Sun 11am–8pm | Tip Bring home some lovely, artisan-made candles and fragrances at
Boho Bungalow (3692 Bohemian Highway, Occidental, www.thebohobungalow.com).

107 — The Washoe House
Black Bart slept here

In the late 1850s, the hilly terrain between Petaluma and Santa Rosa was known for stone quarries, some of which still exist. Stony Point was a stagecoach stop dominated by the Washoe House, a ramshackle hotel with a veranda across the second floor. The building, completed in 1859, was fashioned from redwood lumber and bound with square nails. It housed a butcher's shop, a carriage manufacturer, a post office and general store, and a saloon.

According to local legend, Ulysses S. Grant once gave a speech from the hotel balcony. Black Bart, the 'poetic' highwayman well known as a robber of Wells Fargo stagecoaches around Northern California in the late 18th century, also stayed here. The Washoe's defining moment came in 1865 when a militia of Union soldiers from Petaluma came riding through on their way to avenge President Lincoln's assassination with an attack on Confederate sympathizers in Santa Rosa. They stopped for ale, had another round for the road, and another. This went on for two days until their wives came to retrieve them. Such was "The Battle of the Washoe House." There is also a ghost in residence, a man who committed suicide but remains in good humor.

In 1999, the Washoe House served as a setting for *True Crime*, a film directed by and starring Clint Eastwood.

These days, in the middle of sallow-colored afternoons, often with the scent of smoke from distant forest fires, the 12 stools in the Washoe House tavern are full. A few men wear black cowboy hats. Women in faded tie-dye have tats on the back of their calves. The ceiling is covered with many hundreds of $1 bills, a living tradition to guarantee business in bad times. Live music plays every night. ESPN is on all the time. Conversation runs from vintage clothing to the future of the marijuana industry. Note the vintage Seaburg Electric Upright piano next to the men's room.

Address 2840 Roblar Road, Petaluma, CA 94952, +1 (707) 795-4544, www.facebook.com/ WashoeHouse, info@washoe.house | Getting there By car, from US-101, take exit 479 onto W Railroad Avenue, then turn right onto Stony Point Road and right onto Roblar Road. | Hours Mon–Thu 8am–9pm, Fri 8am–11:30pm, Sat & Sun 7am–9pm | Tip There are several other haunted places in the area, including the Phoenix Theater in Petaluma, which hosts a friendly spirit called Big Chris and several others as well (201 Washington Street, www.petaluma360.com/article/entertainment/phoenix-theater-hauntings).

108__ Wee Golf & Arcade
From cannibals cooking to drowning dinosaur

One of the obligatory summer pilgrimages for San Franciscans is a trip to the Russian River, just west of Santa Rosa, for the day. You can rent a canoe or kayak and spend the next several hours Tom Sawyering on the water. The route is full of beaches, otters, birds, and picnic spots. The water is waist deep.

When you reach Guerneville, you'll often find live music and people in costume, depending on the current festival, along with a popular barbecue truck parked at Pee Wee Golf & Arcade. Pee Wee is close to the river and very much part of the Russian River pilgrimage. Incidentally, if you don't know this bit of kitsch, miniature golf, otherwise known as putt-putt or crazy golf, is the wacky offspring of golf, the sport of kings that began in the Middle Ages when shepherds in Scotland knocked stones down rabbit holes with their staffs. Putt-putt sprang up in London in 1912, and then in Hamburg in 1926, and on through Europe and North America. The first mini golf franchises were in the US.

The game is strictly a putting affair. The surface is carpeted or turf throughout a geometric layout with obstacles, including tubes, ramps, rises, tunnels, and often a slow moving windmill, all designed to prevent your ball from going into the holes. Holes are approximately 10-foot shots. If you're good at billiards, you'll be good at miniature golf. Still, a hole-in-one is difficult.

Pee Wee was built by a welder named Bill Koplin Sr. in 1948, and it has become a community treasure. Its two 18-hole courses are distinguished by oversized, cartoonish animals, including fish, a dinosaur, and two stocky cannibals boiling somebody in a pot. At dusk, one of the courses glows in the dark. The owner lives above the arcade, a former garage with air hockey and other games. The river regularly drowns the place. Once, all you could see was the dinosaur's head, which is 14 feet tall.

Address 16155 Drake Road, Guerneville, CA 95446, +1 (707) 869-9321, www.guernevillepeeweegolf.com | Getting there By car, from US-101, take exit 494 onto River Road and continue 16 miles. Then turn right onto Pocket Canyon Highway, left onto Drake Road, and right to stay on Drake Road. | Hours Daily 11am–10pm | Tip McT's Bullpen is a small, gay sports bar, where you can sing karaoke and play pool (16246 1st Street, Guerneville, www.mctsbullpen.com).

109 __ Willy's America Jeep Restoration
Valhalla for Military Trucks

The prototype of the US Army vehicle known as the Jeep was unveiled in September 1940, a compact, quarter-ton, four-wheel drive, command and reconnaissance vehicle made by Willys, American Bantam Company, and Ford. In Jeep lore, historian Doug Stewart put it this way: "The spartan, cramped, and unstintingly functional Jeep became the ubiquitous World War II four-wheeled personification of Yankee ingenuity and cocky, can-do determination."

One derivation of the word comes from "Eugene the Jeep," a mysterious character in *Popeye* cartoons in the 1930s. Eugene was Popeye's "jungle pet," who could cross dimensions.

The precursor to the SUV, the Jeep was the darling of what might be called the Military Vehicle Collectors Club (MVCC) movement. Military equipment, particularly World War II trucks and planes, are popular collector's items in the US, and there's no better example of this collector culture than at Willys America Jeep Restoration, a nationally known Willys post-war truck restoration shop in Cazadero. Drive down a windy road until you see the town. Look for the post office, and across the street you'll find owner Paul Barry's Valhalla for Jeeps. The spot was once a train station and a sawmill. Barry's specialty is military vehicles made between 1946 and 1964, but other cars and trucks are welcome, notably Jeepsters and Commandos.

From time to time, Barry hosts an event, and aficionados come to enjoy a BBQ burger lunch and discuss the art of restoration, which may begin with an old, dead Jeep parked out in a field. You can bring it into the bay, get all the parts, and then put it all together, making sure everything fits and the tolerances are right. Then take it all apart, sand off the rust and grime, paint each part, and reassemble it. When you've finished, the feeling is sublime.

Address 6152 Cazadero Highway, Cazadero, CA 95421, +1 (707) 632-5258, www.willysamerica.com | Getting there By car, from US-101, take exit 494 west onto River Road/CA-116, continue for 23 miles, and turn right onto Cazadero Highway. | Hours Mon 9am–6pm, Tue–Fri 8:30am–5pm, Sat 9am–noon | Tip The picturesque and historic Cazadero General Store has everything you need, plus delicious sandwiches (6125 Cazadero Highway, Cazadero).

110__Wingo

A ghost town

California is filled with ghost towns, primarily east of the Sierra Nevada. The remains of these places are a measure of the boom-and-bust nature of California, and of the state's vast geological wealth discovered in the 19th century – not just gold and oil, but ores, like cinnabar, opal, and mercury. There are few ghost towns in Northern California, and Sonoma has two of them.

One of those is Mercuryville in the Mayacamas Mountains. The town was last seen alive in the 1960s, when the population sign read "2," referring to the older couple living above the gas station. Such were the last *noire* days of an outpost that once included a popular hot spring and the nearby Socrates mine, which seemed to be an endless trove of exotic minerals. These days, Mercuryville's fame is tied to its proximity to The Geysers, the world's largest geothermal field, which includes a system of 18 geothermal power plants taking in steam from more than 350 wells.

And then there is Wingo, a handful of withered barns and cabins, and a train trestle from the 1800s that still bears the weight of freight trains passing by. The town is set along the Sonoma Creek in the tidal marshlands. It was originally known as Norfolk, a steamship station that sent some trains to Sonoma, others to Calistoga. It was once a very busy town, serving as a stop for steamer passengers from San Francisco to the north.

In 1879, the railroad company changed the town's name to Wingo, though the derivation isn't clear. It may refer to "Wendigo," a native American dark spirit. But by 1937, the Golden Gate Bridge was open, and activity here came to a close. Wingo is particularly popular for photographers. Be mindful of the wooden walkways that are broken in places, and remember that these structures are mostly wooden and built on stilts. Wingo is now part of the San Pablo Bay National Wildlife Refuge.

Address Wingo, Sears Point, Sonoma, CA 95476 | Getting there Wingo can only be reached by foot. Starting at CA-121/Fremont, drive to Carneros Highway and then take Millerick Road. Follow the country road through the sloughs to the gate and bird sanctuary sign. Park and continue on foot a half-mile to the train trestle to Wingo. | Hours Daily dawn–dusk | Tip The San Pablo Bay National Wildlife Refuge is an excellent place to go birdwatching for migratory species, including the largest population of wintering canvasback ducks in the western US (2100 Sears Point Road, www.fws.gov/refuge/san-pablo-bay).

111 The Wolf House
A dream to last 1,000 years

You'll find the ruin of Wolf House down an old macadam lane, or you can walk to the end of a longer, narrow path winding through the forest filled with bronze-colored manzanita, bay, and buckeye trees, various kinds of oaks, an occasional redwood, and pine groves. Signs warn of mountain lions and rattlesnakes, noting that these local residents merely want to be left undisturbed. After half a mile, you'll come to a fork. To the left is a short run up to the grave of author Jack London (1876–1916), a modest plot surrounded by an ancient picket fence. In the middle is a large corundum-colored stone covered in ferns. The stillness here is a bit ironic, considering London's zest for adventure. He once wrote in a letter, "Get up; wake up; kick in; do something; deliver the goods; come across; arise or be forever damned."

Also buried here are the ashes of his spectacular wife Charmian (1871–1955). She was an excellent writer in her own right, but as often happens, she was forgotten in the light of her husband's success. She was his equal in many ways, not least when it came to travel and adventure. When Jack died, she had some much lesser romances, including a brief affair with Harry Houdini.

But the destination here is the ruins of Wolf House. Return to the fork, take the other branch, and a hundred yards further on, you'll arrive. The remains are towering, foreboding, and yet beautiful from certain angles.

Wolf House was a 10-year dream, a 15,000-square-foot mansion with 26 rooms and the latest technology. But in 1913, shortly before the house would have been completed, it burned to the ground. Arson was suspected initially, but paint cloths were more likely the cause. Jack London died three years later. During construction, London wrote, "Act of God permitting, my house will be standing for a thousand years." According to Charmian, he never recovered from the loss.

Address 2400 London Ranch Road, Glen Ellen, CA 95442, +1 (707) 938-5216, jacklondonpark.com, jacklondonpark@jacklondonpark.com | **Getting there** By car, from Sonoma, take Arnold Drive N to Glen Ellen and turn left onto London Ranch Road. | **Hours** Daily 9am–5pm | **Tip** Morton's Warm Springs Resort is a very old fashioned and family-friendly resort (1651 Warm Springs Road, Glen Ellen, www.mortonswarmsprings.com).

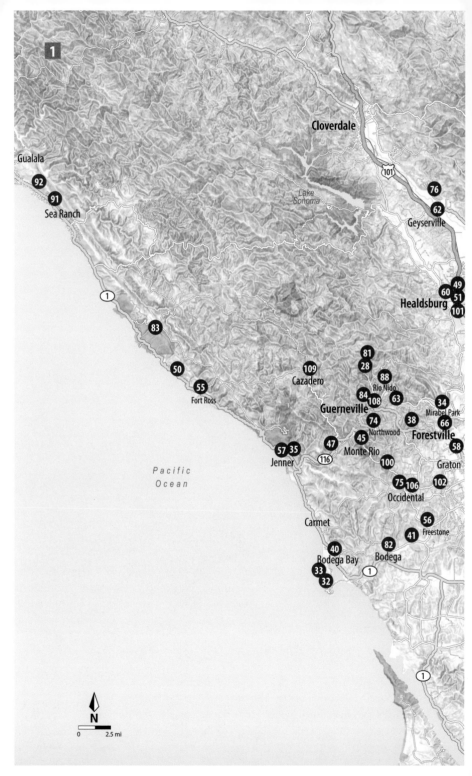

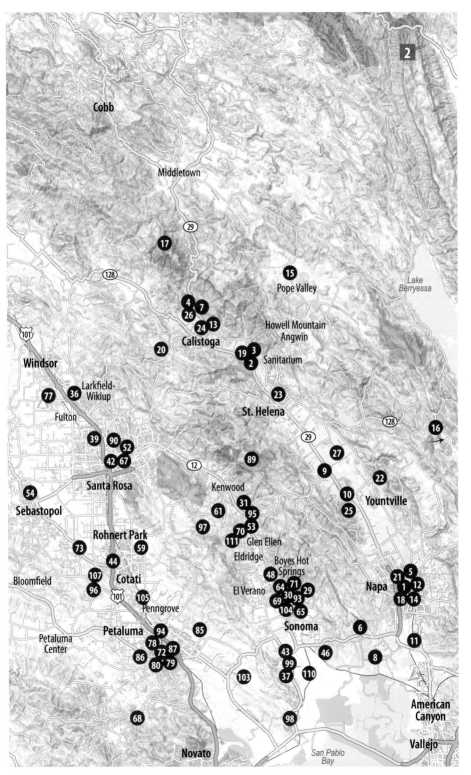

Floriana Petersen, Steve Werney
111 Places in San Francisco
That You Must Not Miss
ISBN 978-3-7408-1698-8

Floriana Petersen, Steve Werney
111 Places in Silicon Valley
That You Must Not Miss
ISBN 978-3-7408-1346-8

Katrina Nattress, Jason Quigley
111 Places in Portland
That You Must Not Miss
ISBN 978-3-7408-0750-4

Harriet Baskas, Cortney Kelley
111 Places in Seattle
That You Must Not Miss
ISBN 978-3-7408-1992-7

Laurel Moglen, Julia Posey,
Lyudmila Zotova
111 Places in Los Angeles
That You Must Not Miss
ISBN 978-3-7408-1889-0

Kelsey Roslin, Nic Yeager,
Jesse Pitzler
111 Places in Austin
That You Must Not Miss
ISBN 978-3-7408-1642-1

Dana DuTerroil, Joni Fincham,
Daniel Jackson
111 Places in Houston
That You Must Not Miss
ISBN 978-3-7408-1697-1

Dana DuTerroil, Joni Fincham,
Sara S. Murphy
111 Places for Kids in Houston
That You Must Not Miss
ISBN 978-3-7408-1372-7

Philip D. Armour, Susie Inverso
111 Places in Denver
That You Must Not Miss
ISBN 978-3-7408-1220-1

Cristyle Egitto, Jakob Takos
111 Places in Palm Beach
That You Must Not Miss
ISBN 978-3-7408-1695-7

Jo-Anne Elikann, Susan Lusk
111 Places in New York
That You Must Not Miss
ISBN 978-3-7408-2057-2

Wendy Lubovich, Ed Lefkowicz
111 Museums in New York
That You Must Not Miss
ISBN 978-3-7408-0379-7

Joe DiStefano, Clay Williams
111 Places in Queens
That You Must Not Miss
ISBN 978-3-7408-0020-8

John Major, Ed Lefkowicz
111 Places in Brooklyn
That You Must Not Miss
ISBN 978-3-7408-0380-3

Kevin C. Fitzpatrick, Joe Conzo
111 Places in the Bronx
That You Must Not Miss
ISBN 978-3-7408-0492-3

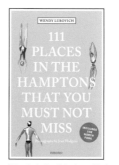

Wendy Lubovich, Jean Hodgens
111 Places in the Hamptons
That You Must Not Miss
ISBN 978-3-7408-1891-3

Brian Hayden, Jesse Pitzler
111 Places in Buffalo
That You Must Not Miss
ISBN 978-3-7408-1440-3

Kim Windyka, Heather Kapplow,
Alyssa Wood
111 Places in Boston
That You Must Not Miss
ISBN 978-3-7408-1558-5

Andréa Seiger, John Dean
**111 Places in Washington
That You Must Not Miss**
ISBN 978-3-7408-1890-6

Kaitlin Calogera, Rebecca Grawl,
Cynthia Schiavetto Staliunas
**111 Places in Women's History
in Washington That You Must
Not Miss**
ISBN 978-3-7408-1590-5

Brandon Schultz, Lucy Baber
**111 Places in Philadelphia
That You Must Not Miss**
ISBN 978-3-7408-1376-5

Allison Robicelli, John Dean
**111 Places in Baltimore
That You Must Not Miss**
ISBN 978-3-7408-1696-4

Amy Bizzarri, Susie Inverso
**111 Places in Chicago
That You Must Not Miss**
ISBN 978-3-7408-1030-6

Amy Bizzarri, Susie Inverso
**111 Places for Kids in Chicago
That You Must Not Miss**
ISBN 978-3-7408-0599-9

Michelle Madden, Janet McMillan
**111 Places in Milwaukee
That You Must Not Miss**
ISBN 978-3-7408-1643-8

Sandra Gurvis, Mitch Geiser
**111 Places in Columbus
That You Must Not Miss**
ISBN 978-3-7408-0600-2

David Doroghy, Graeme Menzies
**111 Places in Vancouver
That You Must Not Miss**
ISBN 978-3-7408-0494-7

Graeme Menzies, David Doroghy
111 Places in Victoria
That You Must Not Miss
ISBN 978-3-7408-1720-6

David Doroghy, Graeme Menzies
111 Places in Whistler
That You Must Not Miss
ISBN 978-3-7408-1046-7

Jennifer Bain, Christina Ryan
111 Places in Calgary
That You Must Not Miss
ISBN 978-3-7408-1559-2

Elizabeth Lenell-Davies,
Anita Genua, Claire Davenport
111 Places in Toronto
That You Must Not Miss
ISBN 978-3-7408-0257-8

Gillian Tait
111 Places in Edinburgh
That You Shouldn't Miss
ISBN 978-3-7408-1476-2

Tom Shields, Gillian Tait
111 Places in Glasgow
That You Shouldn't Miss
ISBN 978-3-7408-2237-8

Gillian Tait
111 Places in Fife
That You Shouldn't Miss
ISBN 978-3-7408-1740-4

John Sykes, Birgit Weber
111 Places in London
That You Shouldn't Miss
ISBN 978-3-7408-1644-5

Ed Glinert, David Taylor
111 Places in Oxford
That You Shouldn't Miss
ISBN 978-3-7408-1990-3

Jonjo Maudsley, James Riley
111 Places in Windsor
That You Shouldn't Miss
ISBN 978-3-7408-2009-1

Michael Glover,
Richard Anderson
111 Places in Sheffield
That You Shouldn't Miss
ISBN 978-3-7408-1728-2

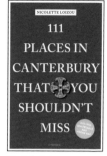

Nicolette Loizou
111 Places in Canterbury
That You Shouldn't Miss
ISBN 978-3-7408-0899-0

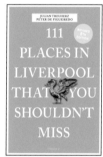

Julian Treuherz,
Peter de Figueiredo
111 Places in Liverpool
That You Shouldn't Miss
ISBN 978-3-7408-1607-0

David Taylor
111 Places in Newcastle
That You Shouldn't Miss
ISBN 978-3-7408-1043-6

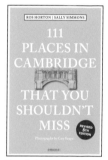

Rosalind Horton,
Sally Simmons, Guy Snape
111 Places in Cambridge
That You Shouldn't Miss
ISBN 978-3-7408-1285-0

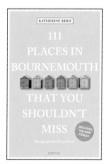

Katherine Bebo, Oliver Smith
111 Places in Bournemouth
That You Shouldn't Miss
ISBN 978-3-7408-1166-2

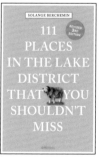

Solange Berchemin
111 Places in the Lake District
That You Shouldn't Miss
ISBN 978-3-7408-1861-6

Alexandra Loske
111 Places in Brighton and
Lewes That You Shouldn't Miss
ISBN 978-3-7408-1727-5

I am extremely grateful to all those who shared their unique stories and secrets of Napa and Sonoma Counties with me. As always, a very special thank you to Mark MacNamara for his major contribution to the writing process, I am so grateful to have you as a dear friend and creative co-writer. Thanks to Achim Mantschaff, who introduced me to the Emons family and team years ago and encouraged me to write the *111 Places* books. I could not have finished the book without the continued support and help of my editor Karen Seiger – thank you. I am very grateful to my partner Steve Werney for taking exquisite photos of these exciting discoveries and to my daughter Adriana Petersen for always inspiring me. xoxo

Photo Credits
All photos by Steve Werney except:
Rancho Obi-Wan (86): Courtesy of Rancho Obi-Wan

Art Credits:
Ars Longa Vita Brevis (ch. 1): Alan Shepp
Bottle House (ch. 6): Mildred Howard
The Grape Crusher Monument (ch. 11): Gino Miles
Vila Ca'toga Artwork (ch. 26): Carlo Marchiori
Erickson Fine Art Gallery (ch. 49): *Dancing Horses I* by Antoinette
Von Grone; *When We Could Fly* and Head by Paul Van Lith;
Elmo by Finley Fryer; Portrait by Carlos Perez
Expanding Universe (ch. 50: Beniamino Bufano
Florence Avenue Art (ch. 54): Brigitte Laurent and Patrick Amiot
Eternity – Myanmar (left), *Shape Shifter – Mongolia* (right) (ch. 65):
Lisa Kristine
Moon House (ch. 70): Douglas Fenn Wilson
Tower (ch. 76): Ann Hamilton
Rhino Redemption (ch. 87): Kevin Clark
Spoonfall (ch. 101): Ned Kahn

Floriana Petersen lives in San Francisco and grew up in Slovenia, where she studied art history and developed a lifelong passion for all things beautiful and unusual. She is a noted interior designer of both residential and commercial spaces. www.forianainteriors.com

Steve Werney grew up in the small town of Clovis, in California's Central Valley, and has called San Francisco home since 1992. A contractor by trade, when he is not building homes, you'll find him "constructing" photographs through the lens of his camera.

Floriana and Steve have also collaborated on top-selling guidebooks *111 Places in San Francisco That You Must Not Miss* and *111 Places in Silicon Valley That You Must Not Miss*.

The information in this book was accurate at the time of publication, but it can change at any time. Please confirm the details for the places you're planning to visit before you head out on your adventures.